ETHICS AND COMPLIANCE

Challenges for Internal Auditing

By
Curtis C. Verschoor,
CIA, CPA, CFE, CMA

The IIA Research
Foundation

Disclosure

Copyright © 2007 by The Institute of Internal Auditors Research Foundation (IIARF), 247 Maitland Avenue, Altamonte Springs, Florida 32701-4201. All rights reserved. Printed in the United States of America. No part of this publication may be reproduced, stored in a retrieval system, or transmitted in any form by any means — electronic, mechanical, photocopying, recording, or otherwise — without prior written permission of the publisher.

The IIARF publishes this document for informational and educational purposes. This document is intended to provide information, but is not a substitute for legal or accounting advice. The IIARF does not provide such advice and makes no warranty as to any legal or accounting results through its publication of this document. When legal or accounting issues arise, professional assistance should be sought and retained.

The Professional Practices Framework for Internal Auditing (PPF) comprises the full range of existing and developing practice guidance for the profession. The IIA's Professional Practices Framework provides guidance to internal auditors globally and paves the way to world-class internal auditing.

This guidance fits into the Framework under the heading Development and Practice Aids.

The mission of The IIA Research Foundation (IIARF) is to be the global leader in sponsoring, disseminating, and promoting research and knowledge resources to enhance the development and effectiveness of the internal auditing profession.

ISBN 978-0-89413-612-2
07587 07/07
First Printing

CONTENTS

FOREWORD

The dynamics of the internal auditing profession were illustrated by two events occurring as this volume went to press. First, The IIA in early 2007 issued an exposure draft of proposed changes to The Professional Practices Framework. The comment period for the first exposure draft ended on April 30, 2007. Major objectives of the initiative included increasing the transparency and flexibility of the guidance development, review, and issuance processes. Additional efforts will be expended in the future to review the content of various Practice Advisories and other guidance to assure that they remain current and up to date. Thus, although the initial changes in the Framework are likely to be relatively minor, a total review of all guidance will take place in the years thereafter.

Secondly, on December 19, 2006, the Public Company Accounting Oversight Board (PCAOB) issued an Exposure Draft of two new auditing standards that would (1) supersede Auditing Standard No. 2 (AS 2) that is discussed in this volume and (2) supersede the current external auditor guidance concerning use of internal auditing in audits of both internal control over financial reporting and financial statements contained in AS 2 and AU 322. The comment period for these exposure drafts ended on February 26, 2007. These two standards are likely to have little direct effect on the practice of internal auditing, except for increasing the potential opportunities for internal auditors to add value to their organizations. Neither of these pronouncements substantially affects the guidance presented in this volume.

The second proposed standard, Considering and Using the Work of Others, is of most interest to internal auditors. It would:

- Allow the [external] auditor to appropriately use the work of others, and not just internal auditors, for both the internal control audit and the financial statement audit, eliminating a barrier to integration of the two audits;

- Encourage greater use of the work of these others by requiring [external] auditors to evaluate whether and how to use their work to reduce auditor testing;
- Require the [external] auditor to understand the relevant activities of these others and determine how the results of that work may affect the audit;
- Provide a single framework for using the work of others based on the auditor's evaluation of the combined competence and objectivity of others and the subject matter being tested; and
- Eliminate the explicit principal evidence provision previously included in AS No. 2.

ABOUT THE AUTHOR

Dr. Curtis C. Verschoor, CIA, CPA, CFE, CMA, is the Ledger & Quill Research Professor in the School of Accountancy and Management Information Systems and Wicklander Research Fellow in the Institute for Business and Professional Ethics, both at DePaul University, Chicago. He is also a research scholar in the Center for Business Ethics at Bentley College in Waltham, Massachusetts, a fellow of the Corporate Governance Center at Kennesaw State University, Kennesaw, Georgia, and an honorary visiting professor in the Centre for Research in Corporate Governance at the Sir John Cass Business School, City University of London. He is a private investor as well as a consultant, author, speaker and expert witness on the subjects of governance, ethics, audit committees, internal controls, and auditing management.

Presently, Dr. Verschoor serves on the board of directors of nonprofit organizations and is a contributing editor for several academic and practitioner journals. He received undergraduate and MBA degrees from the University of Michigan at Ann Arbor, and a doctorate in business from Northern Illinois University.

Prior to his career in academia, his financial career in industry included service as the corporate controller of both the Colgate-Palmolive Company and Baxter International, the CFO of a small diversified public corporation, and the chief internal audit executive of The Singer Company. Previously, he was the national director of education of Touche Ross & Co., a predecessor of Deloitte, LLP.

Dr. Verschoor has been widely quoted in various media, including *The New York Times, Wall Street Lawyer, Houston Chronicle, Chicago Tribune*, and *Dallas Morning News*. He has also written books, monographs, columns, and articles in prominent journals, including: *Journal of Accountancy, Strategic Finance, Directors' Monthly,*

Internal Auditor, Management Accounting, Internal Auditing, Accounting Today, Bank Management, and *CPA Journal.*

His most recent books are *Audit Committee Briefing: Understanding the 21ˢᵗ Century Audit Committee and Its Governance Roles, Governance Update 2003: Impact of New Initiatives on Audit Committees and Internal Auditors,* and *Audit Committee Briefing – 2001: Facilitating New Audit Committee Responsibilities.*

He is an active volunteer in several professional organizations, presently serving on the Professional Conferences Committee of The Institute of Internal Auditors and the Ethics Committee of the Institute of Management Accountants. His biography is contained in the current *Who's Who in America, Who's Who in the Midwest, Who's Who in Education,* and *Who's Who in Finance.*

Dr. Verschoor can be reached at curtisverschoor@sbcglobal.net.

LEGAL DISCLAIMER

This document does not represent legal or professional advice.

This book is intended only as a general educational tool and should not be considered a substitute for professional advice in connection with matters of auditing, ethics, or compliance with various laws, regulations, and rules. It provides information of various levels and types that are applicable in many contexts, but readers are advised to obtain competent counsel in the areas of law, accounting, auditing, and ethics when applying these topics to specific situations. No guarantee of fitness is made concerning the information provided.

While the author and The Institute of Internal Auditors Research Foundation have attempted to provide an accurate and complete product that is up to date as of the date of its publication, errors or omissions may occur. This volume is offered on an "as-is" basis and no express or implied warranties are offered regarding its contents.

Links to third-party Web sites and information cited from third parties were current as of the date of publication of this work, but those third parties may make changes thereafter that may make those links and information obsolete.

CHAPTER 1
INTRODUCTION

Over the last few years, the subject of ethics and compliance in organizations of various kinds and sizes has greatly increased in visibility and importance for practitioners of governance, their advisors and mentors, for monitors of ethics and compliance processes, and for those responsible for oversight. The parade of business scandals and ethical lapses that has seemed to continue without significant letup has led to continued legislative and regulatory mandates for improved governance practices.

As a consequence of these events, many organizations have made significant improvements in their governance structures. Many have come to the realization, sometimes belatedly, that good governance that is founded on a strong ethical climate represents a significant best business practice that benefits all stakeholders. This is true whether the organization is large or small, for-profit or not-for-profit, publicly held, or privately owned. Effective ethics and compliance programs support good governance practices.

In fact, recent research by LRN, a consulting firm specializing in governance, ethics, and compliance management, provides additional evidence that a company's ability to maintain an ethical corporate culture is key to the attraction, retention, and productivity of employees.[1] According to the study, 94% of employees said it was either critical or important that the company they worked for is ethical. This compares with 76% who said so in a similar survey six months earlier. Eighty-two percent said they would prefer to be paid less but work at a company that had ethical business practices rather than receive higher pay at a company with questionable ethics. More than a third said they had left a job because they disagreed with the actions of either fellow employees or managers. This is true across all ages, genders, and socioeconomic factors.

As an important aspect of their organization's governance, internal auditors should be aware of all of these developments and fully familiar with the details of a majority of them so they will be able to apply the concepts and practices they exemplify in all circumstances relevant to their own organizations. Members of audit committees, corporate counsel, and external auditors should also be knowledgeable about matters concerning ethics and compliance, as their responsibilities in ethics and compliance are also increasing.

A recent survey conducted by The IIA reports that 54% of responding internal auditors do not do ethics auditing because it is either "too hard" or "not our job."[2] Major objectives of this handbook are to convince internal auditors of the importance of ethics and compliance systems to effective governance processes, a key responsibility of internal auditing, and also to provide information that will give internal auditors comfort in providing ethics-related services. A recent article in *Internal Auditor* quotes a member of The IIA's Ethics Committee as saying, "An ethics audit uses the exact same processes, interview, and documents as a standard business audit."[3]

A principal reason internal auditors need to be especially well-informed about matters of ethics and compliance is the fact that this subject is critically important to all three of the principal areas of responsibility that are contained in The IIA's definition of internal auditing:

> [Internal auditing] helps an organization accomplish its objectives by bringing a systematic, disciplined approach to evaluate and improve the effectiveness of risk management, control, and governance processes.[4]

One of the most significant business risks facing every organization is the possibility of loss of trust and confidence by investors, customers, vendors, employees, and the public at large. In terms of control, the second area of internal auditing expertise, integrity, and ethical values are known to be the most important components of internal control. While not synonymous, the concepts of governance and that of ethics and compliance are closely intertwined. Internal auditing fulfills an important role in assuring that ethics and compliance programs are properly designed to achieve the objectives for which they were established, and that they continue to operate in an effective manner to assure accomplishment of these goals.

Thus, practitioners of internal auditing, as significant components of governance processes, and also persons in related fields, need to be particularly aware of all developments affecting organizational ethics and compliance. An objective of this book is to help fulfill those needs.

Chapter 2, Ethics and Compliance in Internal Auditing Professional Standards, discusses the numerous references to ethics and compliance processes that are contained in The IIA's *International Standards for the Professional Practice of Internal Auditing (Standards)* and the related Practice Advisories that recommend how they should best be put into practice. The primary professional standard in this regard is Performance Standard 2100, Nature of Work. This standard paraphrases into action requirements the portion of the definition of internal auditing set forth above. Chapter 2 also sets forth internal auditing responsibilities for compliance with The IIA's Code of Ethics.

Chapter 3 is titled Importance of Ethics and Compliance to Internal Control and Risk Management. The chapter presents details of the interrelationships between ethics and compliance and that of internal control. The 1992 COSO *Internal Control – Integrated Framework* report notes the critical importance of the control environment to effective controls. This concept has been carried forward in guidance to external auditors contained in generally accepted auditing standards.

In September 2004, COSO published a counterpart framework to its 1992 internal control document on the subject of risk management titled *Enterprise Risk Management – Integrated Framework*.[5] This document incorporates and expands on COSO's earlier seminal study on the framework of internal control, while providing a more robust and more extensive focus on the broader subject of enterprise risk management.

Chapter 3 also discusses the 2006 COSO publication that reiterates and augments its earlier guidance concerning the importance of ethics and compliance to internal control. This three-volume set is titled *Internal Control over Financial Reporting – Guidance for Smaller Public Companies.*[6] Although directed primarily to smaller companies, much of the content has application to all organizations, including those established as not-for-profit and governmental entities. As the organization's experts in matters of internal control, internal auditors need to be fully familiar with the contents of each of these documents that relate to ethics and compliance and their broader implications.

Chapter 4, Requirements for Ethics and Compliance Contained in Sarbanes-Oxley Legislation, covers the statutory rules and their implementing guidance that requires all publicly held corporations in the United States to establish elements of an effective ethics and compliance program. Emphasis is placed on the related challenges for internal auditing. No counterpart ethics and compliance-related legislation has been enacted in other countries.

The U.S. Sarbanes-Oxley Act of 2002[7] contains a number of such requirements. Section 301 of Sarbanes-Oxley, "Public Company Audit Committees," requires the audit committees of public companies to establish a confidential system for reporting wrongdoing, a key element of an effective ethics and compliance program. Section 406, "Code of Conduct for Senior Financial Officers," requires disclosure of whether a public company has adopted a code of ethics for senior financial officers, and if not, the reason therefore.

Section 302 of Sarbanes-Oxley, "Corporate Responsibility for Financial Reports," requires the principal executive and financial officers to certify in each annual or quarterly financial report that they have designed proper internal and disclosure controls and have evaluated their effectiveness. Section 404, "Management Assessment of Internal Controls," requires public companies to publish management's annual assessment of the effectiveness of the internal control system over financial reporting as well as an attestation by the organization's external auditor of management's assessment. The effective date for the Section 404 requirement to assess internal control over financial reporting and provide an independent auditor attestation has been postponed by the Securities and Exchange Commission (SEC) for smaller public companies.

In 2007, the SEC promulgated conceptual guidance to provide issuers of securities to the public with the principles of how these Sarbanes-Oxley requirements are to be put in practice. As noted above, the most widely accepted COSO internal control framework describes integrity and ethical values as the most important components of an effective internal control system.

Chapter 5, Sarbanes-Oxley Independent Sector Implementation Initiatives, describes follow-on initiatives of Sarbanes-Oxley. The chapter discusses the requirement that the New York Stock Exchange and NASDAQ have published for companies listed on those exchanges to maintain an effective code of conduct for directors, officers, and employees as a condition of continued listing. Stock exchange rules set forth the basic requirements of such codes of conduct.

This chapter also contains portions of the guidance to external auditors contained in Public Company Accounting Oversight Board (PCAOB) Audit Standard No. 2, An Audit of Internal Control over Financial Reporting Performed in Conjunction with an Audit of Financial Statements.[8] Chapter 5 emphasizes the portions of this standard that will best enable internal auditing to provide value in testing internal controls in a manner that can be use to directly assist an external auditor's internal control attestation and audit that is required under Section 404 of Sarbanes-Oxley.

Chapter 6, Ethics and Compliance Requirements Contained in Prominent Best Practice Recommendations, advances other motivations for the establishment of an effective ethics and compliance program and the related internal auditing challenges. The works of two committees of the International Federation of Accountants (IFAC) provide guidance to internal auditors in assisting management to design an effective code of conduct and monitoring its performance as well as providing guidance on helping accountants and auditors to have a strong ethical compass.

Another major topic included in the chapter is a discussion of the 2004 revision to the United States Sentencing Guidelines (USSG) for organizations. The revision places greater emphasis on ethics as a condition of enabling organizations to avail themselves of the mitigating circumstances provisions that are contained in the guidelines. The Sentencing Commission's press release reads:

> Organizations must promote an organizational culture that encourages ethical conduct and a commitment to compliance with the law. In particular, the amendment requires boards of directors and executives to assume responsibility for the oversight and management of compliance and ethics programs. Effective oversight and management presumes active leadership in defining the content and operation of the program. At a minimum, the amendment explicitly requires organizations to identify areas of risk where criminal violations may occur, train high-level officials as well as employees in relevant legal standards and obligations, and give their compliance and ethics officers sufficient authority and resources to carry out their responsibilities.[9]

The 2004 revision to USSG requirements also mandates continuous improvement through risk assessment and analysis. It is clearly evident that these requirements directly involve the internal audit activity.

The following two chapters in the volume discuss aspects of two important components of effective ethics and compliance programs and methods that internal auditors should consider in making assessments of them. Chapter 7, The Role of an Effective Code of Conduct, describes guidance for the characteristics of the content of such codes and also how best they should be put into practice. Coverage includes draft good practice guidance for codes by IFAC.[10] Chapter 8, The Role of an Effective Confidential Reporting Process, discusses the importance and key elements of this aspect of a formal ethics and compliance program. Research has shown that an effective confidential reporting process is one of the most important tools in assuring a strong ethical climate in the organization.

The subject matter of Chapter 9, Assessing Ethics and Compliance Programs, includes the characteristics of effective ethics and compliance programs together with the most efficient and effective methods that internal auditors can use for assessing their quality. The chapter begins with an overall view of how internal auditors have a unique perspective from which to evaluate the ethical culture in their organization. Internal auditors have a significant head start in the area of ethics and compliance through their familiarity with the organization and how it functions.

This final chapter then describes some of the more effective organizational characteristics internal auditors may observe as well as some of the techniques that may be helpful in performing an evaluation. The chapter includes the work of PricewaterhouseCoopers, the Ethics Resource Center, and the Association of Certified Fraud Examiners. This chapter also includes guidance published by the Open Compliance and Ethics Group (OCEG) titled *Measurement & Metrics Guide*.[11] OCEG has also developed an evaluation tool titled "Does the Company Get It? – 20 Questions to Ask Regarding Compliance, Ethics, and Risk Management.[12]

One of the important challenges for internal auditing is to provide services that properly balance the need for independence and objectivity that is necessary to fulfill the assurance requirements of the board of directors, primarily through its audit committee, while at the same time providing value to local management. *Ethics and Compliance: Challenges for Internal Auditing* should assist internal auditors in this critically important area of governance.

References

[1]LRN Press Release, "New Research Indicates Ethical Corporate Cultures Impact the Ability to Attract, Retain and Ensure Productivity Among U.S. Workers," August 3, 2006. www.lrn.com

[2]Jackson, Russell, "Keeping Companies Clean," *Internal Auditor*, December 2006, p. 40.

[3]Id., p. 42.

[4]The Institute of Internal Auditors, *The Professional Practices Framework* (Altamonte Springs, FL: The Institute of Internal Auditors), 2005, p. xxxvii.

[5]Committee of Sponsoring Organizations of the Treadway Commission, *Enterprise Risk Management – Integrated Framework: Executive Summary* (New York: American Institute of Certified Public Accountants), 2004. www.cpa2biz.com

[6]Committee of Sponsoring Organizations of the Treadway Commission, *Internal Control over Financial Reporting – Guidance for Smaller Public Companies: Executive Summary* (New York: American Institute of Certified Public Accountants), 2006. www.cpa2biz.com

[7]P.L. 107-24.

[8]PCAOB, Auditing Standard No. 2, 2004. www.pcaobus.org/Standards

[9]US Sentencing Commission News Release May 3, 2004 "Commission Tightens Requirements for Corporate Compliance and Ethics Programs." www.ussc.gov

[10]IFAC, Defining and Developing an Effective Code of Conduct, Exposure Draft, November 2006. ·
www.ifac.org/PAIB/Committee.php#Guidance

[11]OCEG, *Measurement & Metrics Guide*, OCEG Practice Aid, Exposure Draft, July 2006. www.oceg.org/view/MMG

[12]OCEG, Appendix I to *Internal Audit Guide – Evaluating a Compliance and Ethics Program*, OCEG Practice Aid, Exposure Draft, May 2006. www.oceg.org/view/IAG

CHAPTER 2
ETHICS AND COMPLIANCE IN INTERNAL AUDITING PROFESSIONAL STANDARDS

Ethics and compliance systems are directly involved with all three of the primary areas of emphasis for internal auditors set forth in The IIA's definition of internal auditing: risk management, control, and governance. In addition, compliance with The IIA's Code of Ethics is a critically important requirement for effective internal auditing. The IIA's *International Standards for the Professional Practice of Internal Auditing (Standards)* and related Practice Advisories contain many references to an organization's processes that involve ethics and compliance systems. The *Standards* also set forth the specific responsibilities internal auditors have to provide assurance and consulting services that evaluate and improve the effectiveness of those processes.

The internal auditing responsibilities for performing services relating to ethics and compliance are presented in general terms in Standard 2100, Nature of Work:

> The internal audit activity should evaluate and contribute to the improvement of risk management, control, and governance processes using a systematic and disciplined approach.[1]

Related Practice Advisories set forth recommended best practices endorsed by The IIA for implementing this *Standard*.

Characteristics of Compliance Programs

The first Practice Advisory under Standard 2100 that deals with the subject matter of ethics and compliance is PA 2100-5, Legal Considerations in Evaluating Regulatory Compliance Programs. It describes the purpose of compliance programs is to assist organizations in preventing inadvertent employee violations of laws, regulations, and company policies, detect illegal activities, and discourage intentional employee violations. Regulatory compliance programs can also help prove insurance claims, determine director and officer liability, create or enhance corporate identity, and decide the appropriateness of punitive damages.[2]

PA 2100-5 also sets forth characteristics of an effective compliance program and suggests that a major role for internal auditing is to evaluate their organization's program in light of those attributes. These qualities should also allow the entity's program to comply with the provisions of the U.S. Sentencing Guidelines (see discussion in Chapter 4, Requirements for Ethics and Compliance Contained in Sarbanes-Oxley Legislation).

Internal Auditing Responsibilities

PA 2100-5 also sets forth specific responsibilities for internal auditing. The Practice Advisory states in paragraph 6 that:

> The audit plan should include a review of the organization's compliance program and its procedures, including reviews to determine whether: written materials are effective, communications have been received by employees, detected violations have been appropriately handled, discipline has been evenhanded, whistleblowers have not been retaliated against, and the compliance management has fulfilled its responsibilities. The auditors should review the compliance program to determine whether it can be improved, and should solicit employee input in that regard.[3]

PA 2100-5 also notes that organizations should establish an effective compliance program to be followed by an entity's employees and other agents that are reasonably capable of reducing the prospect of criminal conduct. Characteristics of such a program are set forth in paragraph 2 of the Practice Advisory. They include:

1. The organization should develop a written business code of conduct that clearly identifies prohibited activities. The code should be written in language that all employees can understand, avoiding legalese.

2. A good code provides guidance to employees on relevant issues. Checklists, a question and answer section, and reference to additional sources for further information all help make the code user friendly.

3. Codes of conduct that are viewed as legalistic and one-sided by employees may increase the risk that employees will engage in unethical or illegal behavior, whereas codes that are viewed as values-based, straightforward and fair tend to decrease the risk that employees will engage in such activity.

4. The organization should create an organizational chart identifying board members, senior officers, senior ethics/compliance officer, and others who are responsible for implementing compliance programs.

5. Companies using reward systems that attach financial incentives to apparently unethical or illegal behavior can expect a poor compliance environment.

6. Companies with international operations should institute a compliance program on a global basis, not just selective geographic locations. Such programs should reflect appropriate local laws, regulations, and other conditions.[4]

Specific individual(s) within high-level personnel of the organization should be assigned overall responsibility to oversee regulatory compliance with standards and procedures, as set forth in paragraph 3 of the Practice Advisory:

1. High-level personnel of the organization means individuals who have a substantial control of the organization or who have a substantial role in the making of policy within the organization.

2. High-level personnel of the organization includes: a director; an executive officer; an individual in charge of a major business or functional unit of the organization, such a sales, administration or finance; and an individual with substantial ownership interest.

3. To be fully effective, the CEO and other senior management must have significant involvement in the program.

4. In some organizations, assigning chief compliance responsibilities to the company's general counsel may convince employees that management is not committed to the program and the program is important to the legal department only, not the firm as a whole. In other organizations, the opposite may be true.

5. In a large company with several business units, compliance responsibilities should be assigned to high-level personnel in each unit.

6. It is not enough for the company to create the position of chief compliance officer and to select the rest of the compliance unit. The company should also ensure that those personnel are appropriately empowered and supplied with the resources necessary for carrying out their mission. Compliance personnel should have adequate access to senior management. The chief compliance officer should report directly to the CEO.[5]

The organization should use due care not to delegate substantial discretionary authority to individuals whom the organization knows or should know through the exercise of due diligence have a propensity to engage in illegal activities, as set forth in paragraph 4 of the Practice Advisory.

- Companies should screen applicants for employment at all levels for evidence of past wrongdoing, especially wrongdoing within the company's industry.
- Employment applications should inquire as to past criminal convictions. Professionals should be asked about any history or discipline in front of licensing boards.
- Care should be taken to ensure that the company does not infringe upon employees' and applicants' privacy rights under applicable laws. Many jurisdictions have laws limiting the amount of information a company can obtain in performing background checks on employees.[6]

Paragraphs 5 through 8 of the Practice Advisory cover issues of communication and training related to compliance as well as a confidential reporting system, monitoring and auditing of program effectiveness, and enforcement through appropriate disciplinary action when wrongdoing is discovered. Selected specific action steps include:

- Taking reasonable steps to enforce compliance with the standards and practices that have been communicated. This includes adequate resources for monitoring of effectiveness by internal auditing and the establishment of a "hot line" or "help line" where employees can obtain guidance in making appropriate decisions and also report activity that they believe to be unethical, illegal, or against the company's code of conduct without fear of reprisal.

- Violations of the standards and practices should result in fair, appropriate, and consistent disciplinary action, regardless of the level of the violator. Ignoring wrongdoing by senior management or "big producers" will only encourage others to engage in similar behavior. Disciplinary action should also be taken on those who should have, but did not, detect and report the violation at an earlier time.

- Taking action to communicate effectively its compliance standards and procedures to all employees and other agents by requiring participation in training programs or by disseminating publications that explain in a practical way what is required. All ethics-related documents, such as codes of conduct and human resource policies/manuals, should be readily available to all employees. Organizations should require employees to periodically certify that they have read, understood, and complied with the company's code of conduct.

- If an offense has been detected, the organization should take all reasonable steps to respond appropriately to the offense and to prevent further offenses.

See also the discussion of this subject in Chapter 9, Assessing Ethics and Compliance Programs.

Internal Auditing Responsibilities Relating to Control

Chapter 3, Importance of Ethics and Compliance to Internal Control and Risk Management, discusses the critical importance of the control environment, including integrity and ethical values to establishing and maintaining an effective system of internal control. This chapter covers internal auditing responsibilities related to internal control that are contained in internal auditing professional standards that involve ethics and compliance. They are set forth in general terms in Standard 2120, Control:

The internal audit activity should assist the organization in maintaining effective controls by evaluating their effectiveness and efficiency and by promoting continuous improvement.[7]

Related Performance Standard 2120.A1 provides more specific guidance directly related to ethics and compliance concerning what internal auditing is required to do on the subject of control:

Based on the results of the risk assessment, the internal audit activity should evaluate the adequacy and effectiveness of controls encompassing the organization's governance, operations, and information systems. This should include:

- Reliability and integrity of financial and operational information.
- Effectiveness and efficiency of operations.
- Safeguarding of assets.
- Compliance with laws, regulations, and contracts.[8]

Related Practice Advisory 2120.A1-1, Assessing and Reporting on Control Processes, discusses in paragraph 3 the normal expectations of senior management and the board of directors that:

...the chief audit executive (CAE) will perform sufficient audit work and gather other available information during the year so as to form a judgment about the adequacy and effectiveness of the risk management and control processes. The CAE should communicate that overall judgment about the organization's risk management process and system of controls to senior management and the audit committee.[9]

Because of the importance to internal control effectiveness of integrity and ethical values and their place in the culture of the organization, considerable audit effort should be required to be directed to areas of ethics and compliance. Contents of the COSO pronouncements defining internal control are discussed in Chapter 3, Importance of Ethics and Compliance to Internal Control and Risk Management.

Internal Auditing Responsibilities Relating to Risk Management

Internal auditing responsibilities risk management responsibilities are set forth in general terms in Standard 2110 – Risk Management:

> The internal audit activity should assist the organization by identifying and evaluating significant exposures to risk and contributing to the improvement of risk management and control systems.[10]

Related Practice Advisory 2110-1, Assessing the Adequacy of Risk Management Processes, in paragraph 5 sets forth this responsibility in more specific detail:

> Internal auditors should obtain sufficient evidence to satisfy themselves that the five key objectives of the risk management processes are being met in order to form an opinion on the adequacy of risk management processes.[11]

Internal Auditing Responsibilities Relating to Financial Reporting

Practice Advisory 2120.A1-4, Auditing the Financial Reporting Process, discusses in paragraphs 6 and 10 several implementing audit procedures concerning ethics and compliance that are recommended for internal auditors:

> Paragraph 6. The board or its audit (or other designated) committee should ask the following questions, and the CAE may be expected to assist in answering them:
> (a) Is there a strong ethical environment and culture?

Do board members and senior executives set examples of high integrity?
Are performance and incentive targets realistic or do they create excessive pressure for short-term results?
Is the organization's code of conduct reinforced with training and top-down communication? Does the message reach the employees in the field?
Are the organization's communication channels open? Do all levels of management get the information they need?
Is there zero tolerance for fraudulent financial reporting at any level?[12]

Paragraph 10. Suggested topics that the CAE may consider in supporting the organization's governance process and the oversight responsibilities of the governing board and its audit committee (or other designated committee) to ensure the reliability and integrity of financial reports:

(a) Financial Reporting
Monitoring management's compliance with the organization's code of conduct and ensuring that ethical policies and other procedures promoting ethical behavior are being followed; an important factor in establishing an effective ethical culture in the organization is when members of senior management set a good example of ethical behavior and provide open and truthful communications to employees, the board, and outside stakeholders.[13]

Internal Auditing Responsibilities Relating to Governance

A considerable number of important internal auditing responsibilities described in internal auditing professional standards concern the subject of governance and involve ethics and compliance. They are set forth in general terms in Standard 2130, Governance:

The internal audit activity should assess and make appropriate recommendations for improving the governance process in its accomplishment of the following objectives:

- Promoting appropriate ethics and values within the organization.
- Ensuring effective organizational performance management and accountability.
- Effectively communicating risk and control information to appropriate areas of the organization.
- Effectively coordinating the activities of and communicating information among the board, external and internal auditors, and management.[14]

Related Assurance Performance Standard 2130.A1, provides more specific guidance directly related to ethics and compliance concerning what internal auditing is required to do regarding the subject of governance:

The internal audit activity should evaluate the design, implementation, and effectiveness of the organization's ethics-related objectives, programs, and activities.[15]

Related Practice Advisory 2130-1, Role of the Internal Audit Activity and Internal Auditor in the Ethical Culture of an Organization, provides background and discusses necessary audit procedures concerning ethics and compliance that are recommended for internal auditors to implement Standard 2130 and 2130.A1. The Practice Advisory underscores the importance of organizational culture in establishing the ethical climate of an enterprise and suggests the role that internal auditors could play in improving that ethical climate. Specifically, the Practice Advisory:

1. Describes the nature of the governance process,
2. Links it to the ethical culture of the organization,

3. States that all people associated with the organization, and specifically internal auditors, should assume the role of ethics advocates, and
4. Lists the characteristics of an enhanced ethical culture.[16]

The content of the Practice Advisory is organized into four areas:

1. Governance and Organizational Culture
   - An organization uses various legal forms, structures, strategies, and procedures to ensure that it:
     (a) Complies with society's legal and regulatory rules,
     (b) Satisfies the generally accepted business norms, ethical precepts, and social expectations of society,
     (c) Provides overall benefit to society and enhances the interests of the specific stakeholders in both the long-and short-term, and
     (d) Reports fully and truthfully to its owners, regulators, other stakeholders, and general public to ensure accountability for its decisions, actions, conduct, and performance.

     The way in which an organization chooses to conduct its affairs to meet those four responsibilities is commonly referred to as its governance process. The organization's governing body (such as a board of directors or trustees or a managing board) and its senior management are accountable for the effectiveness of the governance process.

   - An organization's governance practices reflect a unique and ever-changing culture that affects roles, specifies behavior, sets goals and strategies, measures performance, and defines the terms of accountability. That culture impacts the values, roles, and behavior that will be articulated and tolerated by the organization and determines how sensitive — thoughtful or indifferent — the enterprise is in meeting its responsibilities to society. Thus, how effective the overall governance process is in performing its expected function largely depends on the organization's culture.[17]

2. Shared Responsibility for the Organization's Ethical Culture

- All people associated with the organization share some responsibility for the state of its ethical culture. Because of the complexity and dispersion of decision-making processes in most enterprises, each individual should be encouraged to be an ethics advocate, whether the role is delegated officially or merely conveyed informally. Codes of conduct and statements of vision and policy are important declarations of the organization's values and goals, the behavior expected of its people, and the strategies for maintaining a culture that aligns with its legal, ethical, and societal responsibilities. A growing number of organizations have designated a chief ethics officer as counselor of executives, managers, and others and as champion within the organization for "doing the right thing."[18]

3. Internal Audit Activity as Ethics Advocate

- Internal auditors and the internal audit activity should take an active role in support of the organization's ethical culture. They possess a high level of trust and integrity within the organization and the skills to be effective advocates of ethical conduct. They have the competence and capacity to appeal to the enterprise's leaders, managers, and other employees to comply with the legal, ethical, and societal responsibilities of the organization.

- The internal audit activity may assume one of several different roles as an ethics advocate. Those roles include chief ethics officer (ombudsman, compliance officer, management ethics counselor, or ethics expert), member of an internal ethics council, or assessor of the organization's ethical climate. In some circumstances, the role of chief ethics officer may conflict with the independence attribute of the internal audit activity.[19]

4. Assessment of the Organization's Ethical Climate

- At a minimum, the internal audit activity should periodically assess the state of the ethical climate of the organization and the effectiveness of its strategies, tactics, communications, and other processes in achieving the desired level of legal and ethical compliance. Internal auditors should evaluate the effectiveness of the following features of an enhanced, highly effective ethical culture:

  (a) Formal Code of Conduct, which is clear and understandable, and related statements, policies (including procedures covering fraud and corruption), and other expressions of aspiration.
  (b) Frequent communications and demonstrations of expected ethical attitudes and behavior by the influential leaders of the organization.
  (c) Explicit strategies to support and enhance the ethical culture with regular programs to update and renew the organization's commitment to an ethical culture.
  (d) Several, easily accessible ways for people to confidentially report alleged violations of the Code, policies, and other acts of misconduct.
  (e) Regular declarations by employees, suppliers, and customers that they are aware of the requirements

for ethical behavior in transacting the organization's affairs.

(f) Clear delegation of responsibilities to ensure that ethical consequences are evaluated, confidential counseling is provided, allegations of misconduct are investigated, and case findings are properly reported.

(g) Easy access to learning opportunities to enable all employees to be ethics advocates.

(h) Positive personnel practices that encourage every employee to contribute to the ethical climate of the organization.

(i) Regular surveys of employees, suppliers, and customers to determine the state of the ethical climate in the organization.

(j) Regular reviews of the formal and informal processes within the organization that could potentially create pressures and biases that would undermine the ethical culture.

(k) Regular reference and background checks as part of hiring procedures, including integrity tests, drug screening, and similar measures. [20]

See also the discussion of the subject of governance in Chapter 9, Assessing Ethics and Compliance Programs.

Internal Auditing Responsibilities Arising from The IIA's Code of Ethics

The purpose of The IIA's Code of Ethics is to promote an ethical culture in the profession of internal auditing. An ethical culture within internal auditing is a critical necessity because of the trust placed in the profession's objective assurances about risk management, control, and governance. By its actions as well as its words, the internal audit activity must be seen as an example of strong ethics as well as an active promoter of a strong ethical climate within the organization. The Code consists of:

Principles that are relevant to the profession and practice of internal auditing

Rules of Conduct that describe behavior norms expected of internal auditors. These rules are an aid to interpreting the Principles into practical applications and are intended to guide the ethical conduct of internal auditors.[21]

The Principles include the aspects of Integrity, Objectivity, Confidentiality, and Competency:

Integrity — The integrity of internal auditors establishes trust and thus provides the basis for reliance on their judgment.

Objectivity — Internal auditors exhibit the highest level of professional objectivity in gathering, evaluating, and communicating information about the activity or process being examined. Internal auditors make a balanced assessment of all the relevant circumstances and are not unduly influenced by their own interests or by others in forming judgments.

Confidentiality — Internal auditors respect the value and ownership of information they receive and do not disclose information without appropriate authority unless there is a legal or professional obligation to do so.

Competency — Internal auditors apply the knowledge, skills, and experience needed in the performance of internal auditing services.[22]

The Rules of Conduct provide guidance in applying each of these principles. The Code of Ethics should be followed by both individuals and entities that provide internal auditing services, regardless of whether or not they are members of The IIA or possess a professional certification. Noncompliance with the rules of conduct can form the basis for expulsion from The IIA or withdrawal of the Certified Internal Auditor (CIA) designation.

Internal Auditing Responsibilities Arising from the IFAC Code of Ethics

The International Federation of Accountants (IFAC) is the global association for the accountancy profession. Its mission is to serve the public interest by strengthening the profession by encouraging high quality practices by accountants in public practice, industry and commerce, government, and academe. The IIA is an affiliate member of IFAC. The IFAC Code of Ethics was developed by the International Ethics Standards Board for Accountants and serves as a model for the global accountancy profession. Internal auditors should comply with its provisions.

The IFAC Code is in three parts. The first part establishes the fundamental principles of professional ethics for the professional accountant, and provides a conceptual framework for applying them. The other parts illustrate how the conceptual framework is to be applied in specific situations, depending on whether the accountant is in public practice or in business. The conceptual framework provides examples of safeguards that may be appropriate to address threats to compliance with the fundamental principles and also examples of situations where safeguards are not available, hence, the activity or relationship creating the threat should be avoided. There are five Fundamental Principles: Integrity, Objectivity, Professional Competence and Due Care, Confidentiality, and Professional Behavior:

> **Integrity** — A professional accountant should be straightforward and honest in all professional and business relationships.

Objectivity — A professional accountant should not allow bias, conflict of interest, or undue influence of others to override professional or business judgments.

Professional Competence and Due Care — A professional accountant has a continuing duty to maintain professional knowledge and skill at the level required to ensure that a client or employer receives competent professional service based on current developments in practice, legislation, and techniques. A professional accountant should act diligently and in accordance with applicable technical and professional standards when providing professional services.

Confidentiality — A professional accountant should respect the confidentiality of information acquired as a result of professional and business relationships and should not disclose any such information to third parties without proper and specific authority unless there is a legal or professional right to disclose. Confidential information acquired as a result of professional and business relationships should not be used for the personal advantage of the professional accountant or third parties.

Professional Behavior — A professional accountant should comply with relevant laws and regulations and should avoid any action that discredits the profession.[23]

Summary

The Performance Standards and related Practice Advisories contained in The IIA's Professional Practices Framework set forth a great number of challenges for internal auditing to add value to their organization in the area of ethics and compliance. In addition, whether the services provided by the internal audit activity are assurance or consulting, or even some combination of both, all practitioners of internal auditing need to keep in mind the necessity for total compliance with The IIA and IFAC Codes of Ethics as well as all of the IIA Attribute Standards when performing their services.

References

[1]*The Professional Practices Framework* (Altamonte Springs, FL: The Institute of Internal Auditors), 2005, p. 14.
[2]Id., p. 175.
[3]Id., p. 180.
[4]Id., p. 176.
[5]Id., p. 177.
[6]Id., p. 178.
[7]Id., p. 15.
[8]Id., pp. 15, 16.
[9]Id., p. 218.
[10]Id., p. 14.
[11]Id., p. 208.
[12]Id., p. 243.
[13]Id., p. 246.
[14]Id., p. 17.
[15]Id., p. 17.
[16]Id., p. 252.
[17]Id., pp. 252, 253.
[18]Id., p. 253.
[19]Id., p. 254.
[20]Id., pp. 254, 255.
[21]Id., p. xxix.
[22]Id., pp. xxx, xxxi.
[23]IFAC, *Code of Ethics*. www.ifac.org/Ethics/Pronouncements.php

CHAPTER 3
IMPORTANCE OF ETHICS
AND COMPLIANCE TO
INTERNAL CONTROL
AND RISK MANAGEMENT

Various definitions of internal control have been advanced at various times by different groups, including the AICPA and IIA. Currently, the framework most widely accepted in the United States and perhaps globally is that published by the Committee of Sponsoring Organizations of the Treadway Commission (COSO) in 1992, *Internal Control – Integrated Framework.*[1] This organization has also promulgated guidance relating to risk management.

Internal Control, Committee of Sponsoring Organizations (COSO), 1992 Guidance

In the Framework volume of the 1992 COSO guidance, internal control is defined as follows:

Internal control is a process, effected by an entity's board of directors, management and other personnel, designed to provide reasonable assurance regarding the achievement of objectives in the following categories:

- Effectiveness and efficiency of operations
- Reliability of financial reporting
- Compliance with applicable laws and regulations[2]

COSO's framework volume sets forth five components of internal control:

1. Control Environment — The core of any business is its people — their individual attributes, ethical values, and competence.

2. Risk Assessment — The entity must be aware of and deal with the risks it faces. It also must establish mechanisms to identify, analyze, and manage risks.

3. Control Activities — Control policies and procedures must be established and executed to help ensure that the actions necessary to address risks to achievement of the entity's objectives are effectively carried out.

4. Information and Communication — The systems enabling the entity's people to capture and exchange the information needed to conduct, manage, and control its operations.

5. Monitoring — The entire process must be monitored and modifications made so that the system can react dynamically, changing as conditions warrant.[3]

Committee of Sponsoring Organizations (COSO), 2004 Guidance on Risk Management

In September 2004, COSO published a framework document on enterprise risk management as a counterpart to its guidance on internal control. Titled *Enterprise Risk Management – Integrated Framework,*[4] it notes the importance of internal control, but focuses major attention on the subject of risk management. Enterprise risk management consists of eight interrelated components, including the internal environment, which replaces the concept of the control environment. The definition of the internal environment is:

The internal environment encompasses the tone of an organization, and sets the basis for how risk is viewed and addressed by an entity's people, including risk management philosophy and risk appetite, integrity and ethical values, and the environment in which they operate.[5]

Committee of Sponsoring Organizations (COSO), 2006 Internal Control Guidance

In June 2006, COSO augmented its original 1992 guidance on internal control to provide application support targeted toward smaller entities with emphasis on public company assessment of effectiveness of internal controls over financial reporting.[6] Its guidance is generic and applicable to entities of all sizes and types, however. Particularly helpful is its presentation in Volume 2 of the publication of 20 fundamental principles drawn from the original Framework and a description of the principle's related attributes, together with approaches to applying the principle and examples of how the principle can be applied.

Seven of the 20 principles described in the 2006 COSO publication involve the control environment component of internal control, the most of any component and more than twice as many as the average for the remaining components. This reiterates COSO's conviction concerning the importance of the control environment component to effective internal control. The seven principles contained in the control environment component are:

- Integrity and Ethical Values — Sound integrity and ethical values, particularly of top management are developed and understood and set the standard of conduct for financial reporting.
- Board of Directors — The board of directors understands and exercises oversight responsibility related to financial reporting and related internal control.
- Management's Philosophy and Operating Style — Management's philosophy and operating style support achieving internal control over financial reporting.

- Organizational Structure — The company's organizational structure supports effective internal control over financial reporting.
- Financial Reporting Competencies — The company retains individuals competent in financial reporting and related oversight roles.
- Authority and Responsibility — Management and employees are assigned appropriate levels of authority and responsibility to facilitate effective internal control over financial reporting.
- Human Resources — Human resource policies and practices are designed and implemented to facilitate effective internal control over financial reporting.[7]

The attributes set forth by COSO for the first Principle, Integrity and Ethical Values, for example, include:

- *Articulates Values* — Top management develops a clearly articulated statement of ethical values that is understood at all levels of the organization.
- *Monitors Adherence* — Processes are in place to monitor adherence to principles of sound integrity and ethical values.
- *Addresses Deviations* — Deviations from sound integrity and ethical values are identified in a timely manner and appropriately addressed and remedied at appropriate levels within the company.[8]

Volume 2 of the 2006 guidance sets forth approaches to applying each of the principles in the control environment component. These application approaches could well be used as criteria for evaluating the effectiveness of an organization's ethics and compliance program. For example, for the first principle, Integrity and Ethical Values, the COSO guidance sets forth three applications:

Articulating and Demonstrating Integrity and Ethics

The CEO and key members of management articulate and demonstrate the importance of sound integrity and ethical values to employees through their:

- Day-to-day actions and decision-making.
- Interactions with suppliers, customers, and other external parties that reflect fair and honest dealings.
- Performance appraisals and incentives that diminish temptations inconsistent with financial reporting objectives.
- Intolerance of ethical violations at all levels.

Informing Employees about Integrity and Ethics

Management implements mechanisms to inform new employees and remind current personnel of the company's objectives related to integrity and ethics and related corporate values. Such mechanisms include:

- Providing information to new hires emphasizing top management's views about the importance of sound integrity and ethics.
- Periodically providing employees updated information relevant to maintaining sound integrity and ethical values.
- Making ethics guidelines readily available and understandable.
- Including periodic training and other interactive communications to review current and new ethics policies.
- Periodically receiving confirmations from employees on their understanding of key principles.
- Recognizing and rewarding employees' actions that positively reflect sound integrity and ethical values.

Demonstrating Commitment to Integrity and Ethics

Management demonstrates its commitment to sound integrity and ethical values by following a prescribed investigation process and taking appropriate, timely corrective action when possible violations are identified. For example, management:

- Investigates occurrences of possible violations to gain a thorough understanding of issues and circumstances.
- Develops appropriate documentation.
- Remedies the situation in accordance with prescribed company guidelines on a consistent and timely basis.
- Makes company personnel aware that appropriate investigation and corrective actions have been taken.
- Follow up to support continued compliance.[9]

Volume 3 of the 2006 COSO guidance contains evaluation tools for each of the 20 principles. See also the discussion of this subject in Chapter 9, Assessing Ethics and Compliance Programs.

Open Compliance and Ethics Group (OCEG) Risk Guidance

Risk Assessment is an essential component of the Foundation Guidelines put forth by the OCEG, providing an analytical approach that is based on the potential for events to thwart the achievement of the objectives of compliance and ethics program objectives.[10]

Summary

COSO, the most globally widely accepted guidance on the subject of internal control, places considerable importance on the control environment, including integrity, ethical values, management style, and the culture of the organization as it is expressed in its governance processes. Internal auditing is a vital and important component of an organization's governance. As such, it is responsible for assuring that appropriate ethics and compliance programs have been designed and installed, and are effective. In addition, because of the significant benefits accruing to the organization from having an appropriate ethical culture, internal audit activities should advocate and promote a strong ethical climate in their organization.

References

[1]COSO, *Internal Control – Integrated Framework* (New York: AICPA- publisher), 1992.
[2]Id., p. 9.
[3]Id., p. 12.
[4]COSO, *Enterprise Risk Management – Integrated Framework* (New York: AICPA – publisher), 2004.
[5]Id., Executive Summary, p. 3.
[6]COSO, Internal *Control Over Financial Reporting – Guidance for Smaller Companies*, Three Volumes (New York: AICPA - publisher), 2006.
[7]Id., Vol. 2, p. 19.
[8]Id., Vol. 2, p. 20.
[10]OCEG, *Foundation Guidelines*. www.oceg.org/view/Foundation

CHAPTER 4
REQUIREMENTS FOR ETHICS AND COMPLIANCE CONTAINED IN SARBANES-OXLEY LEGISLATION

The first statutory requirements requiring publicly held corporations to either have a code of ethics or publicly disclose why they do not are contained in the U.S. Sarbanes-Oxley Act of 2002. Sarbanes-Oxley also requires establishment of a confidential reporting process for employees and periodic publication of management's evaluation of the quality of internal and disclosure controls. Another Sarbanes-Oxley provision requires management to assess (and the independent auditor of a public corporation to audit) the adequacy of internal controls over financial reporting. The Public Company Accounting Oversight Board (PCAOB) established by Sarbanes-Oxley has issued guidance for external auditor use in attesting to the fairness of management's report and auditing internal controls over financial reporting. The PCAOB guidance for external auditors is discussed in Chapter 5, Sarbanes-Oxley Independent Sector Implementation Initiatives.

As further implementation of the objectives of Sarbanes-Oxley to improve governance, the stock exchanges have mandated requirements for listed companies to have in place a code of conduct covering directors, officers, and employees. Earlier, the Sentencing Guidelines for Organizations issued by the U.S. Sentencing Commission that were adopted in 1991 contained provisions that have motivated well-run organizations to have an effective ethics and compliance program, even though they are not mandatory in a legal sense. Revisions to the

Guidelines adopted in 2004 have heightened the attention to ethics and related responsibilities of boards of directors or comparable oversight bodies. Additionally, prominent study groups have recommended installation of codes of conduct and appropriate enforcement procedures as a best business practice for organizations of all sizes and types. These subjects are discussed in Chapter 6, Ethics and Compliance Contained in Prominent Best Practice Recommendations.

Legislative Requirements of the U.S. Sarbanes-Oxley Act of 2002

One of the enhanced financial disclosures that Sarbanes-Oxley mandated in Section 406, "Code of Ethics for Senior Financial Officers," was that all publicly held corporations have to disclose whether they either have in place a code of ethics for senior financial officers or state why they have failed to do so. The SEC implementing final rule, Release No. 33-8177 on January 24, 2003, expanded this requirement to include the principal executive officer, principal financial officer, and principal accounting officer or controller, or persons performing similar functions.[1] As noted above, the stock exchanges have issued rules implementing this portion of Sarbanes-Oxley that are discussed in Chapter 5. The final SEC rule also expanded the definition of the term "code of ethics" that was set forth in Sarbanes-Oxley to consist of:

Written standards that are reasonably designed to deter wrongdoing and to promote:

- Honest and ethical conduct, including the ethical handling of actual or apparent conflicts of interest between personal and professional relationships;
- Full, fair, accurate, timely, and understandable disclosure in reports and documents that a registrant files with, or submits to, the Commission and in other public communications made by the registrant;
- Compliance with applicable governmental laws, rules, and regulations;

- The prompt internal reporting to an appropriate person or persons identified in the code of violations of the code; and
- Accountability for adherence to the code.[2]

As another part of Sarbanes-Oxley added requirements for audit committees, Section 301, "Public Company Audit Committees," requires publicly held companies to establish procedures for confidential submission of complaints relating to accounting, internal accounting controls, or auditing matters. These procedures should provide for:

- The receipt, retention, and treatment of complaints received by the issuer regarding accounting, internal accounting controls, or auditing matters; and
- The confidential, anonymous submission by employees of the issuer of concerns regarding questionable accounting or auditing matters.[3]

The SEC implementing final rule for Sarbanes-Oxley Section 301, Release No. 33-8220, issued on April 9, 2003, notes benefits expected from audit committee receipt of anonymous complaints. It states:

The establishment of formal procedures for receiving and handling complaints should serve to facilitate disclosures, encourage proper individual conduct, and alert the audit committee to potential problems before they have serious consequences.[4]

Sarbanes-Oxley Requirements Relating to Internal and Disclosure Control

Additional provisions in Sarbanes-Oxley set forth requirements for publicly held companies to take responsibility for the quality of their systems of internal and disclosure controls, and also periodically assert that such systems are effective. Section 302 of Sarbanes-Oxley, "Corporate Responsibility for Financial Reports," requires the principal executive and principal financial officer to certify in each annual or quarterly report:

(1) the signing officer has reviewed the report;

(2) based on the officer's knowledge, the report does not contain any untrue statement of a material fact or omit to state a material fact necessary in order to make the statements made, in light of the circumstances under which such statements were made, not misleading;

(3) based on such officer's knowledge, the financial statements, and other financial information included in the report, fairly present in all material respects the financial condition and results of operations of the issuer as of, and for, the periods presented in the report;

(4) the signing officers —

    (A) are responsible for establishing and maintaining internal controls;

    (B) have designed such internal controls to ensure that material information relating to the issuer and its consolidated subsidiaries is made known to such officers by others within those entities, particularly during the period in which the periodic reports are being prepared;

    (C) have evaluated the effectiveness of the issuer's internal controls as of a date within 90 days prior to the report; and

    (D) have presented in the report their conclusions about the effectiveness of their internal controls based on their evaluation as of that date;

(5) the signing officers have disclosed to the issuer's auditors and the audit committee of the board of directors (or persons fulfilling the equivalent function) —

    (A) all significant deficiencies in the design or operation of internal controls which could adversely affect the issuer's ability to record, process, summarize, and report financial data and have identified for the issuer's auditors any material weaknesses in internal controls; and

(B) any fraud, whether or not material, that involves management or other employees who have a significant role in the issuer's internal controls; and

(6) the signing officers have indicated in the report whether or not there were significant changes in internal controls or in other factors that could significantly affect internal controls subsequent to the date of their evaluation, including any corrective actions with regard to significant deficiencies and material weaknesses.[5]

In its implementing release, No. 33-8124, the SEC makes a point of the omission of any reference to GAAP as a standard of fair presentation of financial position and results of operation as a criterion of adequate disclosure:

The certification statement regarding fair presentation of financial statements and other financial information is not limited to a representation that the financial statements and other financial information have been presented in accordance with "generally accepted accounting principles" and is not otherwise limited by reference to generally accepted accounting principles. We believe that Congress intended this statement to provide assurances that the financial information disclosed in a report, viewed in its entirety, meets a standard of overall material accuracy and completeness that is broader than financial reporting requirements under generally accepted accounting principles. In our view, a "fair presentation" of an issuer's financial condition, results of operations and cash flows encompasses the selection of appropriate accounting policies, proper application of appropriate accounting policies, disclosure of financial information that is informative and reasonably reflects the underlying transactions and events and the inclusion of any additional disclosure necessary to provide investors with a materially accurate and complete picture of an issuer's financial condition, results of operations and cash flows.[6]

The SEC release also differentiates between internal controls and a newly coined term "disclosure controls." The release states:

For purposes of the certification required by Section 302(a)(4) of the Act, we have defined the term "disclosure controls and procedures" to incorporate a broader concept of controls and procedures designed to ensure compliance with disclosure requirements generally.[7]

Sarbanes-Oxley Requirements for Periodic Internal Control Assessment

One of the more controversial, costly, and extensive requirements contained in Sarbanes-Oxley is Section 404, "Management Assessment of Internal Controls." This portion of the statute requires the annual reports to the SEC of public companies to contain a management internal control report together with an external auditor attestation and report on the assessment made by management. The legislative language is quite simple, yet considerable subsequent guidance efforts by the SEC and the PCAOB has been controversial and continues to the date of writing this volume. Section 404(a) states the internal control report shall:

(1) state the responsibility of management for establishing and maintaining an adequate internal control structure and procedures for financial reporting; and

(2) contain an assessment, as of the end of the most recent fiscal year of the issuer, of the effectiveness of the internal control structure and procedures of the issuer for financial reporting.

Section 404(b) sets forth the requirement that the external auditor who issues the audit report for the issuing company shall also attest to, and report on, the assessment made by management.

After considering the views of numerous commentators, the SEC issued implementing release No. 33-8238 effective August 14, 2003. This regulation set forth final rules requiring a company's annual report to include an internal control report by management that contains:

- A statement of management's responsibility for establishing and maintaining adequate internal control over financial reporting for the company;
- A statement identifying the framework used by management to conduct the required evaluation of the effectiveness of the company's internal control over financial reporting;
- Management's assessment of the effectiveness of the company's internal control over financial reporting as of the end of the company's most recent fiscal year, including a statement as to whether or not the company's internal control over financial reporting is effective. The assessment must include disclosure of any "material weaknesses" in the company's internal control over financial reporting identified by management. Management is not permitted to conclude that the company's internal control over financial reporting is effective if there are one or more material weaknesses in the company's internal control over financial reporting; and
- A statement that the registered public accounting firm that audited the financial statements included in the annual report has issued an attestation report on management's assessment of the registrant's internal control over financial reporting.[8]

The SEC release provided no significant additional details concerning the required external auditor attestation.

The SEC Rule 33-8238 referred to above set the effective date for the first required management assertion and external audit firm attestation for accelerated filers (companies whose market value of outstanding common equity held by non-affiliates was more than $700 million at the end of its second fiscal quarter in 2004); as the next fiscal yearend after June 15, 2004.[9] This pronouncement also added to the provisions of Sarbanes-Oxley a provision that companies that are accelerated filers must evaluate and report any change in their internal control over financial reporting that has materially affected or is reasonably likely to materially affect, the company's internal control over financial reporting. Requirements for companies that are not accelerated filers were postponed to the first fiscal year ending on or after July 15, 2007, by SEC Release 33-8618 dated September 20, 2005.[10] In Release No. 33-8760 dated December 15, 2006, the SEC further postponed the effective dates for Sarbanes-Oxley Section 404 implementation. Non- accelerated filers — companies with market capitalization of less than $75 million — must file a management report with auditor attestation for years ending after December 15, 2007. Foreign accelerated filers — market value over $75 million but less than $700 million — must file a management report for years ended after July 15, 2006, and an auditor attestation for years ending after July 15, 2007.[11]

SEC Proposed Interpretive Guidance to Companies Relating to Sarbanes-Oxley Section 404

As noted earlier, in responding to continuing criticism of the cost of implementing Sarbanes-Oxley Section 404, the SEC in December 2006 proposed interpretive guidance urging public companies to adopt a "top-down and risk-based" approach to evaluating internal control over financial reporting. At the date of publication of this volume, more than 200 comment letters had been received and posted by the SEC, indicating the great interest and controversial nature of the SEC proposal. The final pronouncement is not expected to greatly affect the practice of internal auditing as described in this volume, and may increase the opportunities for internal auditors to add greater value to their organization by following the guidance on ethics and compliance that this reference volume contains.

Summary

In some large organizations that may not have had the internal control consciousness that is mandated by Sarbanes-Oxley, the internal audit activity may have been called upon to provide consulting support to management as it prepared its evaluation of the adequacy of the internal controls over financial reporting. IIA professional standards provide that these assignments could impair independence and objectivity to preclude internal auditing from providing assurance to management and the audit committee as to the effectiveness of internal controls over financial reporting. Internal auditors should be cognizant of these exposures when preparing plans for both consulting and assurance engagements.

References

[1]SEC Release 33-8177, "Final Rule: Disclosure Required by Sections 406 and 407 of the Sarbanes-Oxley Act of 2002," B.1.c.
[2]SEC Release 33-8177, "Final Rule: Disclosure Required by Sections 406 and 407 of the Sarbanes-Oxley Act of 2002," B.2.c.
[3]P.L. 107-204, §301.
[4]SEC Release 33-8220, "Final Rule: Standards Relating to Listed Company Audit Committees," II.C.
[5]P.L. 107-204, §302.
[6]SEC Release 33-8220, "Certification of Disclosure in Companies' Quarterly and Annual Reports," B.3.
[7]Id., B.3.
[8]SEC Release No. 33-8238, Final Rule: Management's Reports on Internal Control Over Financial Reporting and Certification of Disclosure in Exchange Act Periodic Reports.

[9]Id.

[10]SEC Release No. 33-8618, Management's Report on Internal Control Over Financial Reporting and Certification of Disclosure in Exchange Act Periodic Reports of Companies That Are Not Accelerated Filers.

[11]SEC Release No. 33-8760, Internal Control Over Financial Reporting in Exchange Act Periodic Reports of Non-accelerated Filers and Newly Public Companies.

CHAPTER 5
SARBANES-OXLEY
INDEPENDENT SECTOR
IMPLEMENTATION
INITIATIVES

A number of independent sector initiatives were set in motion by the passage of the U.S. Sarbanes-Oxley Act of 2002. They included the setting by the stock exchanges of listing requirements relating to audit committees, establishment of codes of conduct, and internal auditing. Additionally, Sarbanes-Oxley also established the Public Company Accounting Oversight Board (PCAOB) to monitor performance of firms that audit the financial statements of public companies, and to set audit and ethics standards governing the practice of auditing public companies.

Stock Exchange Requirements for a Code of Conduct

Both the NASDAQ and the New York Stock Exchanges have expanded the Sarbanes-Oxley requirements for a code of conduct to include all employees and directors of the corporation as well as senior officers. The NYSE rule is most expansive. As a condition of continued listing by a corporation on the NYSE:

> All listed companies must adopt and disclose a code of business conduct and ethics for directors, officers, and employees and promptly disclose any waivers of the code for directors or executive officers.[1]

Internal auditing can provide great value to senior management and the audit committee by providing assurance that the code of conduct in their organization continues to be appropriate and is functioning as intended.

NYSE Specific Requirements

Although not prescriptive in content or mandatory in methodology, the New York Stock Exchange (NYSE) listing requirement that each company must have its own code of business conduct and ethics provides the most extensive guidance concerning recommended code content. The comment to the rule states:

> No code of business conduct and ethics can replace the thoughtful behavior of an ethical director, officer, or employee. However, such a code can focus the board and management on areas of ethical risk, provide guidance to personnel to help them recognize and deal with ethical issues, provide mechanisms to report unethical conduct, and help to foster a culture of honesty and accountability.[2]

According to the NYSE guidance contained in the comment in the Listed Company Manual, the most important topics that should be addressed in a listed company's code of conduct and ethics include:

- **Conflicts of Interest.** A "conflict of interest" occurs when an individual's private interest interferes in any way — or even appears to interfere — with the interests of the corporation as a whole.
- **Corporate Opportunities.** Employees, officers, and directors should be prohibited from (1) taking for themselves personally opportunities that are discovered through the use of corporate property, information, or position, (2) using corporate property, information, or position for personal gain; and (3) competing with the company.
- **Confidentiality.** Employees, officers, and directors should maintain the confidentiality of information entrusted to them... except when disclosure is authorized or legally mandated.
- **Fair Dealing.** Each employee, officer, and director should endeavor to deal fairly with the company's customers, suppliers, competitors, and employees. None should take

advantage of anyone through manipulation, concealment, abuse of privileged information, misrepresentation of material facts, or any other unfair-dealing practice.

- **Protection and Proper Use of Assets.** All employees, officers, and directors should protect the company's assets and ensure their efficient use.
- **Compliance with Laws, Rules, and Regulations.** The company should proactively promote compliance with laws, rules, and regulations, including insider trading laws.
- **Encouraging and Reporting of Any Illegal or Unethical Behavior.** The company should proactively promote ethical behavior. To encourage employees to report violations of laws, rules, regulations, or the code of business conduct, the company must ensure that employees know that the company will not allow retaliation for reports made in good faith.[3]

The commentary to the NYSE rule continues: "Each code of business conduct and ethics must also contain compliance standards and procedures that will facilitate the effective operation of the code. These standards should ensure the prompt and consistent action against violations of the code."[4] Best practice suggests that the internal audit activity should include some level of review of the current content of its organization's ethics and conduct code and assess the effectiveness of compliance procedures in place.

The counterpart rule for NASDAQ is NASD Rule 4350(n), adopted in 2003, that requires each NASDAQ listed company:

> to adopt a code of conduct applicable to all directors, officers, and employees, and to make such code publicly available. The code of conduct must comply with Section 406(c) of Sarbanes-Oxley. At a minimum, the code should address conflicts of interest and compliance with applicable laws, rules, and regulations, with an appropriate compliance mechanism and disclosure of any waivers given to executives and directors.[5]

The SEC Release approving the rule quotes NASDAQ:

> A code of conduct with enforcement measures provides assurance that reporting of questionable behavior is protected and encouraged, and fosters an atmosphere of self-awareness and prudent conduct.

The SEC release issued Nov. 4, 2003, 34-48745 — *NASD and NYSE Rulemaking Relating to Corporate Governance* that approved the NYSE and NASDAQ proposals requiring disclosure of a code of ethics together with appropriate compliance states:

> The Commission believes that requiring listed issuers to adopt a code of conduct should help to foster the ethical behavior of directors, officers, and employees, because directors, officers, and employees will know the standards of conduct expected of them in ethically fulfilling the responsibilities of their positions and will be made cognizant that their activities will be monitored. The Commission also believes that requiring the code of conduct and any waivers of the code for directors and executives to be disclosed will provide shareholders the opportunity to evaluate the quality of the company's code and the ability to scrutinize waivers of its provisions.

NYSE Listing Rule §303A.7(d) adopted at the same time states that every company listed on the NYSE "must have an internal auditing function." Commentary to the Rule states:

> Listed companies must maintain an internal auditing function to provide management and the audit committee with ongoing assessments of the company's risk management processes and system of internal control. A company may choose to outsource this function to a third-party service provider other than its independent auditor.[6]

Provisions in PCAOB Audit Standard No. 2

In March 2004, the PCAOB published the final version of Auditing Standard No. 2 (AS 2), An Audit of Internal Control over Financial Reporting Performed in Conjunction with an Audit of Financial Statements. At the time it released AS 2, the PCAOB made particular reference to the role of internal auditing. The PCAOB strongly recommended that listed companies invest in a strong, capable, and objective internal audit activity.[7] When developing audit plans, the internal audit activity should be cognizant of the assurance being provided by external auditors to avoid overlap.

AS 2 notes the fact that the final standard allows external auditors to place significant but not total reliance on evidence provided by others, including internal auditors.[8] Paragraph 117 of AS 2 states that the extent the external auditor may rely on the work of others, including internal auditors, depends on their "competence and objectivity." Factors affecting the competence of individuals performing tests of controls [that could be used by the external auditor as part of the attestation] are stated in Paragraph 119 of AS 2. These include:

- Their educational level and professional experience.
- Their professional certification and continuing education.
- The supervision and review of their activities.
- The quality of the documentation of their work, including any reports or recommendations issued.
- An evaluation of their performance.[9]

Paragraph 120 states factors concerning the objectivity of individuals performing tests [that could be relied on by the external auditor]. They include:

The organizational status of the individuals responsible for the work of others in testing controls, including —

    a. Whether the testing authority reports to an officer of sufficient status to ensure sufficient coverage and adequate consideration of, and action on, the findings and recommendations of the individuals performing the testing.

    b. Whether the testing authority has direct access and reports regularly to the board of directors or audit committee.

    c. Whether the board of directors or the audit committee oversees employment decisions related to the testing authority.[10]

Paragraph 120 of AS 2 also sets forth policies to maintain the individual's objectivity about the areas being tested. They include:

    a. Policies prohibiting individuals from testing controls in areas in which relatives are employed in important or internal-control sensitive positions.[11]

    b. Policies prohibiting individuals from testing controls in areas to which they were recently assigned or are scheduled to be assigned upon completion of their controls testing responsibilities.[12]

As noted earlier in this volume, in early 2007, the PCAOB began the process of deliberating two new Audit Standards that would supersede AS 2 concerning the external audit of internal control and portions of AU Section 322, titled "Considering and Using the Work of Others in an Audit." At the time of publication of this volume, the PCAOB had received more than 175 comment letters concerning the proposed Standards. This indicates the high level of interest and controversial nature of these issues. The new Standards are expected to increase the opportunities for internal auditors to add value to their organization's implementation of Sarbanes-Oxley provisions by providing assistance in completing the external audit of internal control over financial reporting.

Summary

Internal auditing can provide substantial value to the organizations listed on both U.S. stock exchanges by assuring senior management and the board of directors that effective systems for compliance with the code of conduct are in place and operating effectively. It can also facilitate compliance with Sarbanes-Oxley Section 404 by either providing testing of internal control effectiveness that is satisfactory to the external audit firm so that its scope can be reduced, and/or support management's evaluation of internal control by providing assurance to senior management and the audit committee that the overall internal control structure is operating effectively and efficiently.

References

[1]NYSE, Inc., *Listed Company Manual*, § 303A ¶10 (2003).
[2]Id.
[3]Id.
[4]Id.
[5]*NASDAQ Manual*, Rule 4350 (n).
[6]NYSE, Inc., *Listed Company Manual*, § 303A ¶7(d) (2003).
[7]Author's recollection of comments made by PCAOB Commissioners in public meeting. The comments were never published.
[8]PCAOB Audit Standard No. 2, ¶ 108.
[9]PCAOB Audit Standard No. 2, ¶ 119.
[10]PCAOB Audit Standard No. 2, ¶ 120.
[11]Id.
[12]Id.

CHAPTER 6
ETHICS AND COMPLIANCE REQUIREMENTS CONTAINED IN PROMINENT BEST PRACTICE RECOMMENDATIONS

In Chapter 2 we discussed the global Code of Ethics that has been developed by the International Federation of Accountants (IFAC) for professional accountants employed in industry and commerce, academe, and government as well as those in public practice. Because of internal auditing's need to maintain its independence, the IFAC guidance may be perhaps even more important to internal auditors than to other groups of professional accountants.

One IFAC committee, the International Education Standards Board (IAESB), has developed guidelines designed to help accountants have ethical values. A different IFAC committee has proposed guidelines designed to help organizations define and develop an effective code of conduct. Because of the importance to a successful ethics and compliance program of an appropriate code of conduct and an effective confidential reporting process, these issues are further discussed in Chapter 7, The Role of an Effective Code of Conduct, and Chapter 8, The Role of an Effective Confidential Reporting Process.

IFAC Guides Accountants and Auditors to Develop and Maintain Ethical Values

Ethics research to assist accountants and auditors was undertaken under the auspices of the IAESB, a committee of IFAC. The information paper was titled "Approaches to the Development and Maintenance of Professional Values, Ethics, and Attitudes in Accounting Education Programs." It provides significant insights into helping accountants and auditors have ethical values and also how to bring about an ethical climate in the organization as a whole. Key ethics threats identified by the research supporting the paper are: self-interest, failure to maintain objectivity; improper leadership and poor organizational culture; lack of ethical courage to do what is right; lack of ethical sensitivity; and failure to exercise proper professional judgment.

The IAESB paper provides significant insights into accountants' perceptions of how ethical issues should be addressed, including:

- Ethics should be learned as a form of lifelong professional development.
- Ethics education requires accountants to think critically before making decisions with ethical implications.
- Most respondents disagree with the premise that individuals' ethical standards cannot be changed or improved.
- Ethical behavior can only be maintained where leaders are models of ethical behavior and ethical courage is needed to translate values into action.
- A consensus exists that ethics should be taught both as a separate unit and also as an integrated theme within other units of pre-certification education.[1]

The IAESB research also concluded that education is important and necessary to accomplish the following goals:

- Develop a sense of ethical responsibility in accountants;
- Improve the moral standards and attitudes of accountants;
- Develop the problem-solving skills that have ethical implications; and
- Develop a sense of professional responsibility or obligation.[2]

The overarching mission of the IAESB, which operates independently of IFAC, is to issue standards, discussion papers and studies, and information papers. These publications deal with the proper credentialing of professional accountants, such as The IIA's Certified Internal Auditor (CIA) examination, as well as with improvement in the quality of continuing professional education and development for experienced members of the accountancy profession. All of the work of the IAESB is intended to apply to professional accountants, such as internal auditors.

Underlying the need for professional accountants to have guidance about professional values, ethics, and attitudes is the fact that the actions of all accountants affect others, both within and outside the organization. Professional accountants, particularly internal auditors, interact with other employees that perform functions such as marketing, production, and research. Internal auditors may also have significant dealings with external stakeholders, such as customers, vendors, and other suppliers. These stakeholders and the public at large rely on the ethical integrity of the accountancy profession and its members, including internal auditors, to ensure that their professional responsibilities are upheld.

Values Needed by Professional Accountants

Underlying IAESB's work involving ethics is the output of another IFAC committee, the International Ethics Standards Board for Accountants. This body issued the Code of Ethics for Professional Accountants, most recently in June 2005. The IAESB has used information in this document to create international educational standards (IES). IES Standard No. 4, Professional Values, Ethics, and Attitudes, prescribes the professional values, ethics, and attitudes that professional accountants should acquire during the time leading to their certification.

Internal auditors need to possess these characteristics to an even greater extent than their accounting colleagues. In its paragraphs 4 through 6, IES Standard No. 4 expresses the need for strong ethical standards to enable professional accountants (including internal auditors) to provide high-quality services that are in the public interest. Excerpted paragraphs from this Standard follow:

4. Society has high expectations of the accountancy profession. It is essential for professional accountants to accept and observe ethical principles regulating all their relationships. Professional values, ethics, and attitudes identify professional accountants as members of a profession and should shape everything they do as professionals.

5. Since professional accountants have a role to play in decision making, they need to have a thorough appreciation of the potential ethical implications of professional and managerial decisions. They also need to be aware of the pressures of observing and upholding ethical principles that may fall on those involved in decision-making processes. This is true whether they are working in public practice, industry or commerce, the public sector, or education.

6. Professional accountants operate in a world of change. Good governance, both corporate and public, depends greatly on adherence to professional values, ethics, and attitudes. In such circumstances, a clear understanding of, and education in, ethical principles is essential.[3]

IFAC IES Standard No. 4 states in paragraph 15 that the objectives of the coverage of values and attitudes in the educational programs for professional accountants should lead to a commitment to:

• The public interest and sensitivity to social responsibilities;
• Continual improvement and lifelong learning;
• Reliability, responsibility, timeliness, courtesy, and respect; and
• Laws and regulations.[4]

The contents of educational programs for learning professional values, ethics, and attitudes, according to paragraph 16 of IES Standard No. 4, should include:

- The nature of ethics;
- Differences, advantages, and drawbacks of approaches to ethics that are either detailed and rules-based or more framework oriented;
- Compliance with the fundamental ethical principles of integrity, objectivity, commitment to professional competence and due care, and confidentiality;
- Professional behavior and compliance with technical standards;
- Concepts of independence, skepticism, accountability, and public expectations;
- Ethics and the profession: social responsibility.[5]

The responsibilities of internal auditors to comply with The IIA's Code of Ethics and the provisions of the IFAC Code of Ethics are discussed earlier in Chapter 2.

Importance of Ethics and Compliance in U.S. Sentencing Guidelines

The U.S. Sentencing Commission was created by the Sentencing Reform Act provisions of the Comprehensive Crime Control Act of 1984. The Commission promulgated guidelines for federal court sentencing persons in organizations convicted of crimes. One of the factors that can mitigate punishment that would otherwise be determined is the existence of an effective compliance and ethics program. Its importance to internal auditors is directly influenced by the characteristic of effectiveness set forth in Item 5(A) of the provisions of Chapter 8, Part B of the Guidelines:

The organization shall take reasonable steps —
A) to ensure that the organization's compliance and ethics program is followed, including monitoring and auditing to detect criminal conduct.[6]

The importance of ethics and compliance was enhanced on October 8, 2003, when an Ad Hoc Advisory Group on the Organizational Sentencing Guidelines presented its report recommending improvements designed to:

- Promote an organizational culture that encourages a commitment to compliance;
- Require compliance training at all levels of the organization;
- Define high-level personnel's responsibilities for compliance programs;
- Require programs to provide anonymous reporting mechanisms for potential violations of law; and
- Require ongoing risk assessments as an essential component of the design, implementation, and modification of an effective program.[7]

The final report of the Ad Hoc Advisory Group was submitted to Congress April 30, 2004, and accepted later in that year.[8] The revised requirements that have been put into effect place greater emphasis on instilling and maintaining an ethical culture in the organization. Concerning this point, the Sentencing Commission press release reads as follows:

Organizations must promote an organizational culture that encourages ethical conduct and a commitment to compliance with the law. In particular, the amendment requires boards of directors and executives to assume responsibility for the oversight and management of compliance and ethics programs. Effective oversight and management presumes active leadership in defining the content and operation of the program. At a minimum, the amendment explicitly requires organizations to identify areas of risk where criminal violations may occur, train high-level officials as well as employees in relevant legal standards and obligations, and give their compliance and ethics officers sufficient authority and resources to carry out their responsibilities.[9]

The 2005 *Sentencing Commission Manual* sets forth in Chapter 8 requirements of an effective compliance and ethics program, noting that an organization shall:

- Exercise due diligence to prevent and detect criminal conduct, and
- Otherwise promote an organizational culture that encourages ethical conduct and a commitment to compliance with the law.[10]

The *Manual* goes on to state that:

- Such compliance and ethics program shall be reasonably designed, implemented, and enforced so that the program is generally effective in preventing and detecting criminal conduct.[11]

The *Manual* states that an effective compliance and ethics program must include:

(1) Standards and procedures to prevent and detect criminal conduct;

(2) High-level oversight, responsibility and authority, adequate resources and direct access to the governing authority;

(3) Screening of personnel to eliminate those having previous illegal conduct;

(4) Communication of program to and training at all levels;

(5) Auditing, monitoring, and evaluating program effectiveness;

(6) Non-retaliatory internal reporting systems;

(7) Discipline and incentives to promote compliance; and

(8) Upon detection of a violation, take reasonable steps to respond to and prevent further similar offenses.[12]

Internal auditors can provide significant value to their organizations by evaluating on behalf of management and the board as to whether the necessary elements of an effective compliance program are actually in place and operating properly. In this way, the organization may better avail itself of the mitigating circumstances provisions that are contained in the sentencing guidelines.

Summary

As noted in earlier chapters, the ethical climate in the organization is important to the achievement of many management objectives, including the management of risks, controls, and governance processes. Internal auditors should be at the forefront of their organizations' efforts to establish and maintain an ethical climate through their participation in assessing the effectiveness of the ethics and compliance program.

References

[1]IAESB Press Release, August 14, 2006, p. 5.
www.ifac.org/MediaCenter/
[2]IAESB, "Approaches to the Development and Maintenance of Professional Values, Ethics, and Attitudes in Accounting Education Programs," Information Paper, pp. 53, 54.
www.ifac.org/Education/Pronouncements.php
[3]IAESB IES Standard No. 4, p. 60.
www.ifac.org/Education/Pronouncements.php
[4]Id., p. 62.
[5]Id., pp. 62, 63.
[6]*U.S. Sentencing Guideline Manual*,§8B2.1.(b)(5) (2005).
[7]U.S. Sentencing Commission, Report of the Ad Hoc Advisory Group on the Organizational Sentencing Guidelines, Oct. 7, 2003.
[8]U.S. Sentencing Commission News Release May 3, 2004, "Commission Tightens Requirements for Corporate Compliance and Ethics Programs."
[9]Id.
[10]*U.S. Sentencing Guideline Manual*, §8B2.1.(a) (2005).
[11]Id.
[12]*U.S. Sentencing Guideline Manual*, §8B2.1.(b) (2005).

CHAPTER 7
THE ROLE OF AN EFFECTIVE
CODE OF CONDUCT

Previous chapters described several legal requirements and various governance recommendations for an organization to have a code of conduct, a keystone part of every ethics and compliance program. This chapter describes more specific direction as to appropriate contents of an effective code of conduct, together with guidance on its development and implementation.

Code of Conduct

A code of conduct necessarily serves as the core of an effective ethics and compliance program. Earlier chapters have set forth the code of conduct or ethics requirements in the U.S. Sentencing Guidelines, Section 406 of the U.S. Sarbanes-Oxley Act of 2002, and the New York Stock Exchange, as well as the recommendations published by IFAC. Each organization, however, is obligated to design systems and processes to best achieve these legal and best practice objectives in accordance with its own culture, structure, size, and management style.

Regular internal audits of the organization's ethics and compliance program add great value to the organization. Internal auditing serves as the cornerstone of management's assessment of internal control over financial reporting, as required by Section 404 of Sarbanes-Oxley. Internal auditing also provides assurance to the audit committee regarding its responsibilities for oversight of the organization's confidential reporting system, as required by Section 301 of Sarbanes-Oxley. Finally, internal auditors provide assurance concerning the organization's code of ethics as required by the stock exchanges or Sarbanes-Oxley's Section 406. Many companies have decided to develop a separate code of ethics for their senior executive and senior financial officers. Assessing the effectiveness of this tool requires a separate audit.

IFAC Good Practice Guidance Relating to Codes of Conduct

In November 2006, the IFAC Professional Accountants in Business Committee (PAIB) re-exposed for additional public comment its earlier Good Practice Guide *Defining and Developing an Effective Code of Conduct*.[1] This document emphasizes the benefits of an organization having an effective code as a key element of good governance. Research shows employees prefer to work for entities having strong core values and ethics together with a commitment to live up to them, leading to better productivity, lower personnel turnover with lower training costs, reduced risk of fraud and other legal action.

The PAIB proposed guidance also points out the importance of ethics and compliance to internal control, and professional accountants should be able to accomplish objectives in the following areas:

- Recognition of potential ethics problems and provision of methods for their disposition
- Articulation of the framework within which ethics can be considered in decision-making and resolution of ethical conflicts
- Identification of the expectations of stakeholders and the implications of meeting those expectations
- Monitoring and reporting on compliance with their organization's code of conduct
- Assessing whether proposed action on current and future initiatives effectively manages the risks faced by the organization[2]

Seven key principles in defining and developing a code of conduct are set forth by the PAIB document:

- The organization's overarching objective should be to develop a values-based entity, promoting a culture that encourages employees to "do the right thing" and allows them to make appropriate decisions.
- A code of conduct reflects organizational context. There is no "one size fits all" even in the same industry.
- Commitment from the board of directors: ultimately, ethical responsibility lies with the board of directors (or its equivalent), the body that has the power to influence an organization's culture and behavior. Boards should specifically oversee the development of the code of conduct (and a wider ethics and values program) and formally appoint a senior manager to supervise that development.
- A multidisciplinary and cross-functional group should lead code development. This group should strive for substantial consensus in setting standards and priorities.
- Clearly identifying the established process for code development will promote wider understanding of, and agreement on, the key stages and activities.
- A code should apply across all jurisdictions.
- Continuous awareness and enforcement of the code and the wider compliance and ethics program is an important part of conveying management's commitment to their underlying principles. A continuous awareness program should sustain interest in and commitment to the code. Employees and others should be made aware of the consequences of breaching the code.[3]

Additional Code of Conduct Guidance

The Ethics Resource Center (ERC), a not-for-profit organization that conducts research to help strengthen the character of business and provide benchmarks for evaluating ethics and compliance programs, recommends that a code of conduct be of reasonable length, not so long and legalistic that it won't get read. According to the ERC, its contents should include:

- Memorable title.
- Leadership letter.
- Table of contents.
- Introduction-prologue.
- Credo.
- Core values.
- Code-provisions — substantive matters.
- Information and resources.

The ERC believes that the steps necessary to develop an effective code include:

- Planning the work effort.
- Collecting data.
- Writing the draft code.
- Specifying reporting and enforcement mechanisms.
- Having the code reviewed.
- Obtaining board approval.
- Choosing communication and education strategies.
- Scheduling code updates.

The Open Compliance and Ethics Group (OCEG) provides guidance as to an organization's code of conduct:

An organization should adopt and maintain a code (or codes) of conduct tailored to its particular business needs and culture. Although the terms are different, the content and purpose of these instruments are sufficiently similar — they act as a set of principles to guide individual conduct. A code is particularly powerful when internal controls are weak, incomplete, or nonexistent — and for the countless occasions when individuals encounter the unexpected or undefined risk.

An organization must do more than issue a written code of conduct that sits on a shelf. The code, and compliance with its terms, must be managed and monitored to ensure the principles and practices established by the code are honored and observed within the organization. The organization must demonstrate enforcement of the code.

Principles

- Participation from multiple stakeholders
- Participation from multiple levels of the organization
- Understandable
- Addresses all legal mandates and requirements
- Addresses voluntary policies and values[4]

An attorney author, Steven R. Barth, sets forth the following subject categories that should be contained in a code of conduct:

- Ethical treatment of your customers
- Ethical treatment of your suppliers
- Ethical treatment of your company
- Ethical treatment of your competitors
- Ethical treatment of your fellow employees
- Ethical treatment of your community
- Your ethical obligations of confidentiality
- Your ethical obligations to comply with the law
- Your ethical obligations to maintain your company's financial integrity
- Your ethical obligations with respect to political activities
- International business ethical considerations[5]

Contents of Google, Inc. Code of Conduct

Google notes that its motto is "Do No Evil." The entire contents of the Google, Inc. Code of Conduct are attached as Exhibit A. The document is organized into eight subheadings, of which the first, "Serving Our Users," states the organization's core values — Usefulness, Honesty, Responsiveness, and Taking Action. The remaining topics are:

- Respecting Each Other.
- Avoiding Conflicts of Interest.
- Preserving Confidentiality.
- Maintaining Books and Records.
- Protecting Google's Assets.
- Obeying the Law.
- Using Our Code.[6]

Google, Inc. is a unique organization with a culture that is different from most others. Its Code of Conduct illustrates that fact and demonstrates how an organization can tailor its Code to fit its personality, core values, and DNA. It also shows how the Code can be useful in informing the entire organization of the important aspects of the values that underlie the organization's business strategies and tactics.

Summary

An organization's code of conduct forms an important part of its ethics and compliance program. A clear and concise presentation of business conduct rules that are lived up to by senior and operating management and understood by all and enforced evenly throughout the organization will help employees, suppliers, and other stakeholders recognize ethical and legal issues when they arise. It will also provide a framework for making appropriate decisions. Having proper facilities to deal with ethical dilemmas and potential illegalities will result in lower risks and improved productivity.

Internal auditors should ensure that their organization has spent the necessary time and effort to develop a workable code that will be effective in assuring an ethical culture and compliance with corporate policies, laws, and regulations. They should also be sure that it is properly enforced throughout the organization.

References

[1]PAIB, Defining and Developing an Effective Code of Conduct, Exposure Draft, November 2006.
www.ifac.org/PAIB/Committee.php#Guidance
[2]Id., p. 4.
[3]Id., p. 6.
[4]OCEG, *Foundation, PR2.1 Develop Code of Conduct*.
www.oceg.org/view/Foundation
[5]Steven R. Barth, *Corporate Ethics: The Business Code of Conduct for Ethical Employees*, Aspatore Books, 2003.
[6]www.google.com/conduct.html

CHAPTER 8
THE ROLE OF AN EFFECTIVE
CONFIDENTIAL REPORTING
PROCESS

As noted in earlier chapters of this volume, provisions of the U.S. Sentencing Guidelines and Sarbanes-Oxley as well as best business practices all require organizations to have help/hot lines in place where employees can find assistance in dealing with potential ethically compromising situations or report possible wrongdoing without fear of reprisal. An effective confidential reporting system is the keystone of an effective ethics and compliance program.

Research on Help/Hot Lines

In its 2006 *Report to the Nation on Occupational Fraud & Abuse*,[1] the Association of Certified Fraud Examiners (ACFE) noted that tips from employees were the most common means by which occupational fraud was detected. The ACFE believes that an effective confidential reporting system should extend to third parties, such as customers and vendors.[2] A comparison of frauds in organizations that did have fraud hot lines with those that did not showed that those without hot lines had per scheme losses of twice the size of those in organizations that did. Further, organizations without fraud hot lines took 1.6 times as long to detect the wrongdoing as did organizations with hot lines.

Another research project, the 2006 Corporate Governance and Compliance Hotline Benchmarking Report,[3] was accomplished by The Network, Inc., a provider of ethics and compliance hot line programs and the CSO Executive Council (composed of senior security officers). Some of the findings include:

- 65% of reports received are considered serious enough to warrant an investigation.
- 46% of reports resulted in an investigation with some corrective action taken.
- 10% of reports relate to corruption and fraud issues.
- 54% of individuals using the hot line preferred to remain anonymous.
- Only 20% of individuals reporting observance of wrongdoing state they had previously notified management of the issue.

Network's CEO, Tony Malone, asserts:

> Understanding your organization's ethics program is a crucial part of any business, and the hot line plays a key role in assessing the health of that organization.[4]

Interaction of Hot/Help Lines with Risk Management

Alice Peterson, president of Syrus Global, a Chicago-based provider of services that advance organizational ethics, notes the interaction of information available from hot line systems to risk management in the broadest sense. In her article, "Looking for Risk in all the Right Places," she states that "Anonymous reporting is an undiscovered asset to internal auditors that helps them obtain a valuable view of enterprise risk."

Ms. Peterson concludes that there are significant benefits to the discreet use of confidential communications systems, even in the best managed organizations that have a completely open and trusting culture. She states:

> By enabling anyone any time to report something safely, management and boards can tap into the "water cooler" and can better operate and oversee a well-run enterprise.

To those with some responsibility for operating an anonymous reporting system, she notes that:

This approach not only provides you with a snapshot of enterprise risk, it can also show you how well or poorly your organization is managing those risks.[5]

Summary

An effective confidential help/hot line is critically important to the success of an organization's ethics and compliance program. The key to an effective confidential reporting system is its ability to obtain truthful and complete information from individuals because they are comfortable in providing such information. In other words, little use of a confidential system is not necessarily a sign that an ethical climate does exist in the organization. It may indicate that employees, suppliers, and others are afraid to tell the emperor that he is wearing no clothes.

References

[1]ACFE, 2006 ACFE REPORT TO THE NATION on Occupational Fraud & Abuse, a supplement to *Fraud Magazine*, 2006.
[2]Id., p. 29.
[3]ReportLine Press Release, "The Network, Inc. and CSO Executive Council Announce First Ever Hotline/Helpline Benchmarking Report," 15 November 2006, www.reportline.net
[4]Id.
[5]Alice Peterson, "Looking for Risk in All the Right Places," *Internal Auditing*, September/October 2006, pp. 3 - 16.

CHAPTER 9
ASSESSING ETHICS AND
COMPLIANCE PROGRAMS

Several techniques are available to internal auditors for assessing the effectiveness of an organization's ethics and compliance program and its principal output, an ethical climate that helps to avoid ethical missteps by management and other employees. Further, if ethical misdeeds do occur, an effective ethics and compliance program motivates individuals to report potential transgressions before they escalate in scope. Some assessment methods are formal, whereas others are quite informal. Use of one or a combination of methods depends on the entity's management structure and philosophy. The first portion of the contents of this chapter is adapted from the contents of the author's article titled "The Ethical Climate Barometer."[1]

Internal Auditing Overall Assessment

One key indicator of an organization's ethical climate and effectiveness of its ethics and compliance program can be found in how the internal audit activity actually operates within the organization structure:

- Does the board, audit committee, and senior management fully embrace the activity's mission and respect the contribution it makes to the organization? Does the remainder of the organization?
- Is the activity adequately resourced to accomplish its mission?
- Does the activity offer a systematic, disciplined approach that evaluates and results in improvement to the effectiveness of risk management, control, and governance processes?

Internal auditing's ability to totally fulfill an appropriate mission while openly practicing the core values of the organization provides a deep and ongoing confidence among the internal audit staff and management that the ethical culture of the organization is sound. This informal evaluation should support additional, more formal evaluations that can be communicated to senior management and the audit committee.

Presence of Ethical Factors

Although a continuing informal "attitude review" by the organization's internal audit activity is a good indicator of the lack of ethical difficulties, auditors should periodically make a more formal assessment of the company's ethical culture. One method internal auditors can employ is to determine how many important ethical features of healthy organizations their organization possesses. The following factors are widely recognized as important to that determination:

- *Unquestioned Integrity at All Levels*
  The characteristics of honesty, consistency of policy application, and transparency are all aspects of a strong ethical climate. They lead to an attitude and approach of trust that is absolutely essential in today's technologically oriented business environment. Achieving integrity and consistency through frequent communication and continuous reinforcement of the ethical values that are contained in a code of conduct is essential to maintenance of a strong ethical climate in the organization. Actions speak much louder than words.

- *Collaboration and Holistic Thinking*
  Parochial approaches and turf wars for recognition of the contribution of one segment create distrust and smother full achievement of organization goals. Integrating the latest ideas and the best people from all disciplines into collaborative teams tends to multiply the strength of an organization as a whole.

- *Accountability and Personal Responsibility*
  An ethical culture has a focus on "fixing the problem" rather than "fixing the blame." An attitude of avoiding responsibility

leads to denial and cover up instead of to correcting the offending process or product. Teamwork results in the best long-term solution, not just the most expedient one.

- *Accepting Mistakes and Learning from Them*
  Punishing those willing to take risks but make honest mistakes tends to stifle innovation in others. Learning lessons from mistakes encourages healthy creativity and allows benefits to flow from mistakes. Sports coaches emphasize that losses are a better teacher than victories.

- *Commitment to "Be the Best We Can Be"*
  Mediocrity is easy to achieve, but superior performance requires hard work. Best-in-class organizations continuously engage in improving their processes and practices. The internal audit activity should be a leader in constant improvement and use its ability to spread best practices on an organization-wide basis.

The more widespread the existence of these characteristics within an organization, the higher the possibility there is an inspiring, values-based and shared mission at the core of the organization. The presence of these characteristics also suggests that the organization's leadership is competent and committed to achieve that mission.

Interviews, Surveys, and Focus Groups

Other effective tools for measuring the corporate climate are employee interviews, attitude surveys, and focus groups. Survey questions need only elicit agreement or disagreement responses to issues such as:

- ABC is serious about acting in strict accordance with the core values it sets forth.
- My co-workers and I share the same core values as ABC.
- I believe my personal behavior has a direct influence on ABC's reputation for integrity.

- I have witnessed no violations of the ABC Code of Conduct during the past year.
- I am confident that anything I report to the confidential reporting system will not be used to retaliate against me in any way.
- If I report something to the confidential reporting system, it will be taken seriously, investigated thoroughly, and resolved appropriately.

Administered periodically and always confidential, such surveys provide additional support to the internal auditors' assessment of employee attitudes and perceptions about the organization's management style, ethical climate, code of conduct, and confidential reporting system. Focus groups and employee surveys should always be implemented by independent professionals to help preserve confidentiality and best allow measurement of variability within the organization.

Other Assessment Methods

Additional evidence of a strong ethical culture in the organization can be gathered by internal auditing by analyzing the organization's personnel practices to determine whether they help enable employees to contribute to a positive corporate ethical climate. Internal auditors should consider whether pre-hire background checks and other investigations include drug screening, integrity tests, prior convictions, and similar measures. Because internal auditors have their fingers on the ethical pulse of the organization, any conclusions drawn from this information should be compared with ongoing perceptions gained from audits throughout the organization.

The chief audit executive (CAE) should periodically evaluate the organization's promotion, compensation, and other reward systems to ascertain whether any formal or informal biases exist that could undermine the ethical culture. It is not enough to give lip service to the core value of integrity if senior management turns a blind eye. Finally, the audit committee should ensure that the board compensation committee is aware of any achievement pressures that could be created by any performance incentive programs it may approve.

Internal Auditors' Unique Ethical Responsibilities

As a practical measure, being alert to the ethical pulse of the organization's culture should be an integral part of every audit. Auditors should listen carefully and evaluate critically what they hear from executives, managers, and employees. They should consider putting into their report anything that could represent a compromise of the commitment to act in accordance with the organization's stated mission and core values or code of conduct and ethics.

As internal auditors must possess a high level of trust and integrity to accomplish their mission, they must also serve as effective ethical role models who advocate appropriate conduct at all levels of the organization. They should make proper disclosures of inappropriate, unethical, or illegal conduct to their CAE whenever it comes to their attention. Internal audit activities must ensure that procedures exist to investigate relevant allegations of misconduct and report findings. Professional practitioners of internal auditing do not have the luxury of just "going along" with something they know to be wrong.

In short, individuals who provide internal auditing services have unique ethical responsibilities in that they must act in compliance with the profession's code of ethics as well as that of their own organization. They must apply the principles of integrity, objectivity, confidentiality, and competency to all aspects of their relationships with the audit committee, management, suppliers, and employees.

What Internal Auditors Need to Look For

PricewaterhouseCoopers has set forth eight good governance practices for internal auditors to look for when they are assessing an organization's cultural standards and ethics processes and identifying any governance-related weaknesses.[2] They are:

- Formal written code of conduct
- Clear statement of the organization's cultural and ethical objectives
- Effective communication of the code of conduct, expectations of compliance, and the penalties for violation
- Use of a needs analysis to determine the effectiveness of ethics-related communications and to identify training needs
- Unimpeded and widely available communications channels for use in reporting code of conduct violations
- Required individual confirmation of accountability
- Consistent, effective investigation and enforcement regardless of the status of the individual involved
- Clear management commitment to support oversight activities, including adequate resources and disciplined measurement of governance-related events and activities[3]

Performance Measurement and Metrics

The Open Compliance and Ethics Group (OCEG) has published guidelines for measuring the performance of a compliance and ethics program.[4] This document emphasizes the importance of the ethical culture in the organization. Measurement of effectiveness should be focused on objectives and outcomes. These include:

- Enhance culture of trust, accountability, and integrity.
- Prevent noncompliance.
- Prepare for the time when noncompliance occurs.
- Protect from negative consequences when noncompliance occurs.
- Detect noncompliance.
- Response to noncompliance.

- Improvement in the program to better prevent, protect, prepare, detect, and respond to noncompliance.
- Stakeholder satisfaction.[5]

OCEG believes the objectives of an effective ethics and compliance program should support the organization's business objectives. The program should also identify the boundaries of legal and ethical behavior, and establish a system to alert management when the organization is getting close to (or crossing) a boundary or approaching an obstacle that prevents it from achieving an objective. Importantly, the OCEG guidance suggests that management must be prepared to respond quickly and appropriately to minimize the impact on the organization once a significant ethical issue is identified.

Internal Auditing Guidance by OCEG

Periodic internal audits should provide the board of directors and senior management with an evaluation of the design adequacy and operating effectiveness of the organization's ethics and compliance program. Periodic evaluations should supplement the ongoing monitoring of ethics and compliance incidences and the responses they initiated. Internal auditing assurance to the board also supports the board's responsibility under the U.S. Sentencing Guidelines to ensure that an ethical culture exists within the organization.

To assist the internal audit activity in this task, OCEG has developed an evaluation tool titled "Does the Company Get It? – 20 Questions to Ask Regarding Compliance, Ethics, and Risk Management."[6] The 20 questions are divided into six sections: organizational culture, scope and strategy, structure and resources, management of policies and training, internal enforcement, and evaluation and continual improvement efforts. Each section contains Why Ask This Question?, Potential Answers, and Red Flags. This tool is a part of the OCEG Internal Audit Guide.

Indicators of a Healthy Ethical Climate

The global employee research and consulting firm, ISR,[7] has developed an ethics monitoring tool that focuses on the assessment of the three most important indicators of a healthy ethical climate. They are:

Company Values
- Values — The core values are clear and appropriate, fully embraced and practiced by employees.
- Openness — People speak up without fear and challenge tradition.
- Integrity — The organization operates with integrity, internally and externally.

Internal Policies
- Communication — Information about the organization (e.g., vision, goals, future) is shared, accurate, and timely.
- Enforcement — Processes are in place to report and respond to unethical behavior.
- Employee Relations — Performance is evaluated fairly and diversity is respected.

External Relationships
- Citizenship — The organization acts responsibly toward the environment and the community.
- Marketplace/Customer Relations — Products are safe, competitive practices are fair.
- Investor Relations — Information provided to investors is accurate, timely, and complete.[8]

ISR notes that when employees in financially successful organizations are asked questions around these issues, they have significantly more positive views than their counterparts in organizations that are less financially successful. This helps to build the business case for creating and maintaining an ethically sound organization. Internal auditing can add value by assessing the ethical climate and making recommendations for improvement when required. ISR also notes that an organizational culture in which ethical behavior is both preached and practiced consistently is much less likely to spawn serious breaches of ethical conduct.[9] In other words, the risk of an ethical scandal is much less in an organization with a strong ethical culture.

Resisting Corruption

The Conference Board published the results of its global ethics and compliance benchmarking survey in 2006.[10] It lists five steps toward anti-corruption systems that work:

Step One: High-level Commitment
Step Two: Detailed Statements of Policies and Operating
              Procedures
Step Three: Training and Discussion
Step Four: Hot Lines and Help Lines
Step Five: Investigative Follow-Up[11]

Outcomes that Help Determine the Success of an Ethics and Compliance Program

The nonprofit Ethics Resource Center periodically surveys ethics and compliance in the workplace. The latest (2005) National Business Ethics Survey (NBES)[12] notes that outcomes of the effectiveness of ethics and compliance programs generally declined since 2003, the date of the prior survey. The outcomes are:

- *Misconduct observed by employees* — 52% observed at least one example of misconduct.
- *Willingness of employees to report misconduct* — Of those observing misconduct, only 55% reported it to management.
- *Pressure to engage in unethical conduct* — 10% feel such pressure always or fairly often.

- *Satisfaction with organizational response to reports of misconduct* — When employees perceive that others are held accountable for their actions, their overall satisfaction increases by 32 percentage points.

The NBES report also notes that an ethical culture is a strong deterrent to misconduct. Employees in organizations with strong ethical cultures and a fully developed ethics and compliance program are 36 percentage points less likely to observe misconduct than those in organizations with a weak culture. NBES concludes that ethics and compliance programs are likely to be an essential element in the maintenance of a strong ethical culture.

Anti-fraud Measures

Presence of fraud at any level is a strong indication that the ethics and compliance program has not been effective, according to the association of Certified Fraud Examiners (ACFE). The mission of this organization is to reduce the incidence of fraud and white-collar crime and assist ACFE members in its detection and deterrence. The organization has developed a free *Fraud Prevention Check-up*.[13] This process requires internal auditors or others to determine a fraud prevention score ranging from 0 to 100 for the organization. The evaluator assigns points to seven fraud prevention processes, with the number of points dependent on whether the process is not in place (0 points) to fully implemented, tested within the past year, and working effectively (10 to 30 points, depending on the process).

The ACFE has a considerable number of articles that suggest best practices for fraud prevention and detection. The organization also provides sample forms, checklists, and other tools helpful to internal auditors.

Critical Elements of an Organizational Ethical Culture

The Ethics Resource Center (ERC) research in 2006 found that three ethics-related actions in the workplace have an especially large impact on the effectiveness of an ethics and compliance program. They are:

- Setting a good example,
- Keeping promises and commitments, and
- Supporting others in adhering to ethics standards.[14]

According to Patricia Harned, president of the ERC, the research shows that actions do speak louder than works, and "to create a positive ethical culture, management needs to make sure that employees see their superiors and peers demonstrating ethical behavior in the work they do and decisions they make every day."[15]

Summary

In order to accomplish an effective assessment of the quality of any process, internal auditing must first establish appropriate success criteria. Objectives of this volume include describing sources that will enable internal auditors to first, understand the critical importance that ethics and compliance programs have in today's environment, and second, to begin to have the comfort necessary to provide assurance and consulting services dealing with specific aspects of ethics and compliance programs. These sources should also demonstrate effectiveness criteria for measuring internal auditing assurance services as well as implementation steps designed to assist in consulting services.

The ethical climate and other "soft" ethical controls are so important to the control environment that they deserve a considerable share of auditor attention. Because of the legal and stock exchange requirements that mandate careful consideration of the organization's ethical climate, its assessment should rightfully receive the highest audit priority. Starting with top management, internal auditors can assist in placing emphasis on communicating and modeling those behaviors that demonstrate the organization's core values.

References

[1]Curtis Verschoor, "The Ethical Climate Barometer," *Internal Auditor*, October 2004, pp. 48 – 53.

[2]PricewaterhouseCoopers, *Strengthening Internal Auditing's Role in Corporate Governance*, March 2004.

[3]Id., p. 10.

[4]OCEG, *Measurement & Metrics Guide,* OCEG Practice Aid, Exposure Draft, July 2006. www.oceg.org/view/MMG

[5]Id.

[6]OCEG, Appendix I to *Internal Audit Guide – Evaluating a Compliance and Ethics Program*, OCEG Practice Aid, Exposure Draft, May 2006. www.oceg.org/view/IAG

[7]ISR, "How to Create an Ethical Organizational Culture," White Paper, 2006, www.isrinsight.com

[8]Id., p. 3.

[9]Id., p. 1.

[10]The Conference Board, *Resisting Corruption: an ethics and compliance benchmarking survey*, Research Report R-1397-06 (New York: Conference Board), 2006.

[11]Id., p. 3.

[12]Ethics Resource Center, *How Employees View Ethics in Their Organizations, 1994 – 2005* (Washington, DC: Ethics Resource Center), 2005. www.ethics.org/research/nbes-2005.asp

[13]ACFE, *Fraud Prevention Check-Up,* www.acfe.com/documents

[14]Ethics Resource Center, Critical Elements of an Organizational Ethical Culture, 2006.
www.ethics.org/erc-publications/organizational-ethical-cultural.asp

[15]Ethics Resource Center Press Release "New Research Identifies Three Workplace Actions That Contribute Most to Employee's Ethical Behavior and Compliance," December 15, 2006.
www.ethics.org/about-erc/press-releases.asp

EXHIBIT A
GOOGLE, INC.
CODE OF CONDUCT

Preface

Our informal corporate motto is "Don't be evil." We Googlers generally relate those words to the way we serve our users — as well we should. But being "a different kind of company" encompasses more than the products we make and the business we're building; it means making sure that our core values inform our conduct in all aspects of our lives as Google employees.

The Google Code of Conduct is the code by which we put those values into practice. This document is meant for public consumption, but its most important audience is within our own walls. This code isn't merely a set of rules for specific circumstances but an intentionally expansive statement of principles meant to inform all our actions; we expect all our employees, temporary workers, consultants, contractors, officers, and directors to study these principles and apply them to any and all circumstances which may arise.

The core message is simple: Being a Googler means holding yourself to the highest possible standard of ethical business conduct. This is a matter as much practical as ethical; we hire great people who work hard to build great products, but our most important asset by far is our reputation as a company that warrants our users' faith and trust. That trust is the foundation upon which our success and prosperity rests, and it must be re-earned every day, in every way, by every one of us.

So please do read this code, then read it again, and remember that as our company evolves, the Google Code of Conduct will evolve as well. Our core principles won't change, but the specifics might, so a year from now, please read it for a third time. And always bear in mind that each of us has a personal responsibility to incorporate, and to encourage other Googlers to incorporate, these principles into our work and our lives.

Table of Contents

I. Serving Our Users

Google has always flourished by serving the interests of our users first and foremost. Our goal is to build products that organize the world's information and make it accessible to our users. Here are several principles that all Googlers should keep in mind as we work toward that goal.

a. Usefulness

Our products, features and services should make Google more useful for our users, whether they're simple search users or advertisers, large companies or small companies. We have many different types of users but one primary goal for serving them all. "Is this useful?" is the one question every Googler should keep in mind during every task, every day.

b. Honesty

Our communications with our users should be appropriately clear and truthful. Our reputation as a company that our users can trust is our most valuable asset, and it is up to all of us to make sure that we nourish that reputation.

c. Responsiveness

Part of being useful and honest is being appropriately responsive: recognizing relevant user feedback when we see it, and doing something about it. We take pride in responding to communications from our users, whether in the form of comments, questions, problems, or compliments.

d. Taking Action

Saying that Google, and the products and services we produce, should be useful, honest, and responsive is one thing; achieving that goal 100 percent of the time is, of course, quite another. That means that improving our work over time is largely contingent on the vigilance of our staff. Any time you feel our users aren't being well served, don't hesitate to bring it to the attention of the appropriate person. Googlers don't sit back and say nothing when the interests of our users are at stake. When you feel it's warranted, we encourage you to take a stand.

II. Respecting Each Other

Google is committed to maintaining a supportive work environment in which all employees reach their fullest potential as participants in and contributors to our shared endeavor. To this end, every Googler is expected to do his or her utmost to promote a respectful workplace culture that is free of harassment, intimidation, bias, and discrimination of any kind. If you know of a situation in which you feel these conditions aren't being met, you should immediately report the facts of the situation to your supervisor or the Human Resources Department or both. The important thing is that you bring the matter to Google's attention promptly, so that any concern about discrimination or harassment can be investigated and addressed appropriately.

a. Equal Opportunity Employment
Google is an equal opportunity employer. Employment here is based solely upon one's individual merit and qualifications directly related to professional competence. We don't discriminate on the basis of race, color, religion, national origin, ancestry, pregnancy status, sex, age, marital status, disability, medical condition, sexual orientation, gender identity, or any other characteristics protected by law. We will also make all reasonable accommodations to meet our obligations under the Americans with Disabilities Act (ADA) and state disability laws.

b. Harassment and Discrimination
Google is committed to maintaining a workplace environment free from discrimination and harassment. In keeping with this policy, Google strictly prohibits unlawful discrimination or harassment of any kind, including discrimination or harassment on the basis of race, color, veteran status, religion, national origin, ancestry, pregnancy status, gender, sex, age, marital status, disability, medical condition, sexual orientation, gender identity, or any other characteristics protected by law.

We strictly prohibit all forms of unlawful harassment on the part of all employees, temporary workers, independent contractors, interns, and other professional service providers. We prohibit unlawful harassment in any form, including verbal, physical, or visual harassment.

Sexual harassment includes, but isn't limited to, making unwanted sexual advances and requests for sexual favors where (1) submission to such conduct is made an explicit or implicit term or condition of employment or (2) submission to or rejection of advances is used as the basis for employment decisions affecting an individual, including granting of employee benefits. Sexual harassment also includes unwanted conduct that has the purpose or effect of substantially interfering with an individual's work performance or creating an intimidating, hostile, or offensive working environment, even if it does not lead to tangible or economic job consequences.

If you believe you've been harassed by anyone with whom you come into contact at Google, you must immediately report the incident to your supervisor, Human Resources, or both. Similarly, supervisors and managers who know of any such incident must immediately report the harassment to Human Resources, which will promptly and thoroughly investigate any complaints and take appropriate corrective action when it is warranted. Employees who are found to have violated this Code are subject to discipline up to and including immediate discharge.

As with all other provisions of this Code, retaliation for reporting any incidents of discrimination or harassment or perceived discrimination or harassment, for making any complaints of discrimination or harassment, or participating in any investigation of incidents of discrimination or harassment or perceived discrimination or harassment is strictly prohibited. If a complaint of retaliation is substantiated, appropriate disciplinary action, which may include discharge, will be taken.

Too often one hears stories of employees who were harassed, often for long periods of time, but didn't feel comfortable coming forward. We want to make entirely clear that Google is not, and never will be, the kind of company in which any employee should ever feel that way. If you feel there's a problem, please let us know about it immediately so that any concern of discrimination or harassment can be investigated and addressed promptly and appropriately.

c. Drug and Alcohol Use

Our position on substance abuse is quite simple: it is incompatible with our employee's health and safety, not to mention their chances of long-term success with this company. Employees who are under the influence of alcohol or drugs while on the job can endanger themselves and others and create serious disruptions. So, while any Googler who has cracked opened a beer at a Google-sponsored event, such as at a Friday afternoon TGIF, knows that the legal consumption of alcohol by adults isn't absolutely prohibited on the Google campus, moderation and personal responsibility are the touchstones that should govern the consumption of alcohol while on Google property/worksites, attending a Google-sponsored event, or on company business. Alcohol use that leads to impaired performance or inappropriate behavior, endangers the safety of anyone, or violates the law is strictly prohibited. With regard to drugs, Google strictly prohibits the use, manufacture, possession, purchase, sale or distribution of any illegal drug or controlled substance while on Google property/worksites, attending a Google-sponsored event, or performing company business.

In cases where an employee's manager has reasonable suspicion to believe that the employee is under the influence of drugs and/or alcohol and such influence may adversely affect the employee's job performance, safety, or the safety of others in the workplace, the employee's manager may request an alcohol and/or drug screening for the employee. A reasonable suspicion is based on objective symptoms such as factors relating to the employee's appearance, behavior, speech, etc.

As a condition of employment, Google requires each employee to abide by the terms of this policy and notify the company of any criminal drug statute conviction within five days of such conviction. Each employee will be provided a copy of this policy and will be required to acknowledge that they have reviewed this policy.

Employees who violate Google's substance abuse policy are subject to discipline up to and including termination and, in certain situations, may be subject to civil or criminal penalties.

d. Weapons and Workplace Violence

Google's commitment to providing all our employees with a completely safe work environment extends to any and all forms of weapons and workplace violence. Google will not tolerate any level of violence, or the threat of violence, in our workplace. Under no circumstances should any employee bring any sort of weapon to work or threaten violence of any kind; violations of this policy will result in appropriate disciplinary action, up to and including dismissal. As with other elements of this Code, if you become aware of any violation of Google's weapons and workplace violence policy, you should report it to the Human Resources department immediately. In the case of potential violence, contact Google Security at 650-623-5555.

e. Our Dog Policy

Google's respect and affection for our canine friends is an integral facet of our corporate culture.

We have nothing against cats, per se, but we're a dog company, so as a general rule we feel cats visiting our campus would be fairly stressed out.

III. Avoiding Conflicts of Interest

A conflict of interest occurs when, because of your role at Google, you are in a position to influence a decision or situation that may result in personal gain for you or your friends or family at the expense of the company or our users. All of us at Google should avoid situations that present actual or apparent conflicts of interest; it is our responsibility to act at all times with the best interests of Google and our users in mind. In no way should you personally profit from transactions based on your relationship with Google if it harms the company.

Being open and honest about the possibility of a given conflict of interest is the key to ensuring that it doesn't become a problem. If you're ever in doubt about whether a given action or decision would or wouldn't represent a conflict of interest, please consult your manager or Google's Compliance Program Management Office beforehand.

a. Openness

You should consider it your responsibility to promptly disclose any interest you may have that could conflict with the interests of Google. For example, if one of your family members (including your parents, siblings, children, or in-laws) is or becomes a Google supplier, customer, partner, or competitor, that may not necessarily represent a conflict of interest, but, nonetheless, the right thing to do is to let your manager know about the situation immediately.

One way to consider whether a given action, relationship, gift, etc. constitutes a conflict of interest is to imagine you are at a company meeting. Could you justify your actions in front of your peers? The answer to that question should help you evaluate the situation.

b. Personal Investments

You should not invest, without approval from the Audit Committee of our Board of Directors, in a Google customer, supplier, partner, or competitor if it's at all likely that your investment could compromise the fulfillment of your responsibilities as a Googler. As a general rule, the greater your responsibilities at Google, the more they relate to the relationship between Google and the customer, supplier, partner, or competitor and the larger the amount of the desired investment, the more likely it is that you're doing something that actually or apparently conflicts with the company's interests. When in doubt about whether a personal investment creates an actual or apparent conflict of interest, you should always discuss the situation with your manager or Google's Compliance Program Management Office before making the investment.

c. Gifts and Entertainment

You should not accept any significant gift, payment, or anything else of value from customers, vendors, consultants, partners, or anyone else doing business with Google if the gift would likely be perceived as unduly influencing your business decisions or otherwise creating an actual or apparent conflict of interest. Not all gifts and entertainment necessarily represent conflicts of interest; inexpensive "token" gifts, infrequent and moderate business meals and entertainment, and invitations to events like ball games, celebratory meals, and such can be considered ordinary aspects of many Googlers' business relationships, provided that they aren't excessive or create the appearance of impropriety. Accepting an invitation to a cocktail party thrown by an advertising partner, for instance, might be considered not only an acceptable business activity but a necessary one for an AdWords sales employee. Similarly, accepting a company T-shirt or coffee mug isn't likely to change your assessment of a potential business relationship. However, tickets to something like the Olympics, Super Bowl or World Cup, especially if travel and lodging are included, are in that "gray zone" where it is important to carefully think about the context. Always ask your manager for approval when accepting these and any other significant gifts and entertainment, and don't hesitate to raise any questions or concerns you may have with the Compliance Program Management Office. Gifts of cash or cash equivalents are never permitted.

You should also be appropriately cautious when giving gifts. Google competes for business on the merits of our products, services and people, and never through the offering of improper payments, including gifts or entertainment. In fact, it's worth remembering that many of the companies with whom you have professional dealings will have gifts-and-entertainment policies of their own — many more restrictive than Google's. Be sensitive with regard to any gift you're about to give, including invitations to events, and if you think the gift you're contemplating giving might fall into that "gray zone," it's probably worth checking with your business counterpart to be sure he or she isn't, even inadvertently, violating his or her own company's policy.

d. Business Relationships
Like many of the other situations described in this Code, business relationships that you pursue outside your work at Google require above all your good faith and common sense. As a rule, professional relationships with companies that compete with Google create at least the appearance of a conflict of interest and should be avoided. Accepting personal employment or fees of any kind from any Google supplier, customer, or partner can also create conflicts with your job responsibilities at Google, especially if your job responsibilities relate in any way to the relationship between the supplier, customer, or partner and Google. Before accepting

personal employment or fees from a Google supplier, customer, or partner, you should review the arrangement with your manager and, if necessary, Google's Chief Compliance Officer.

Google employees, including our senior executives, sometimes get the opportunity to serve on other companies' boards. We aren't against this as a matter of principle, but a few words of caution are in order. For one, no Google employee should ever serve as a board member for a company that directly competes with Google. In addition, becoming a board member of a company that is a Google supplier, customer or partner can present greater potential conflict of interest issues than accepting personal employment or fees from such a company. Before you join the board of a Google supplier, customer or partner, you must make sure you receive prior approval from Google's Chief Compliance Officer or General Counsel. Additionally, Google officers must review any outside board memberships with the Chief Compliance Officer or General Counsel before accepting.

It's also important to point out that business opportunities discovered through your work at Google belong first and foremost to Google; you should not pursue such an opportunity yourself unless you first disclose it fully to and receive permission to pursue it from Google's Chief Compliance Officer or General Counsel.

e. Friends and Relatives
Similarly, business relationships with friends and relatives whose interests may conflict with Google's can easily leave you with the sort of conflict of interest that can be difficult to resolve happily. Our rule here is simple: you should not enter into a Google-related business relationship with a close relative, friend or significant other, or a business they manage or control, without first contacting our Chief Compliance Officer or General Counsel. This includes, but is not limited to, appointing him, her or the business as an auditor or outside counsel, or otherwise engaging him, her or the business as a vendor or supplier of goods or services to Google.

IV. Preserving Confidentiality

As we all know, our company's confidential and proprietary information is an invaluable asset that all Googlers must take great care to protect;

company information that leaks prematurely into the press or to competitors can hurt product launches, eliminate our competitive advantage, and prove costly in any number of other ways. So our responsibilities in this arena extend beyond merely not revealing confidential Google material — they also include the proper labeling, securing, and disposal of confidential Google material; the safeguarding of confidential information that Google receives from third parties under non disclosure agreements; and internal compliance with applicable intellectual property laws, such as those protecting patents, copyrights, trade secrets, and trademarks.

The key to exercising proper vigilance in safeguarding confidential Google material is to be sure you know the proper rules of conduct in advance. To whatever extent your particular job involves dealing with confidential information, please be sure you've read the following guidelines, and bear them in mind in the course of your business dealings.

Please remember that the consequences of disclosing confidential or proprietary information can be severe, including dismissal, civil lawsuits against you (by us or others) with significant claims for, among other things, monetary damages, and/or criminal prosecution.

a. Confidential Google Information

Google's "confidential information" may include financial information, product information, user information, etc. The first rule is pretty simple: it is your responsibility to exercise all due care to ensure that confidential company material stays that way. At times, however, some particular project or negotiation properly necessitates disclosing confidential information to a third party. Disclosure of confidential information should be on a "need to know" basis. When such instances arise, be sure to first contact the Legal Department so they can draft an appropriate nondisclosure agreement for the signature of all appropriate parties. In addition, please promptly report to our Legal Department any possible infringements of Google intellectual property.

There are, of course, "gray areas" in which you will need to apply your best judgment. Suppose, for instance, that a friend who works at a non-profit charitable organization asks you for advice about how to improve that site's Google search ranking? Using your Googler knowledge to give your friend site-optimization tips that he or she could have found in any number of books, articles and websites isn't likely to be problematic, but giving tips that aren't publicly known definitely would be. As always, your own judgment is likely to be your best barometer — make sure you use it.

Finally: it's a small world (especially here in Silicon Valley), and some of us will undoubtedly find ourselves involved in personal relationships with people employed by one of our competitors. In this case, as in most others, common sense applies: you shouldn't tell your significant other anything the company considers confidential, any more than you'd reveal that information to a stranger at a coffee shop (and you shouldn't solicit confidential information about the competing company, either).

b. Trademarks, Logos and Copyrights

The name Google Inc., the names of numerous Google products and services, and the various logos related to those products and services are all the company's intellectual property, and unauthorized use of them can do real damage to our company's public image. So it's important to remember that any use of Google logos and trademarks must be cleared in advance by our Marketing Director.

c. Google Partners

Just as you should be careful not to disclose confidential Google information, it's equally important not to disclose any confidential third-party information with which you may be entrusted in the course of your work. You should take care not to accept any confidential information from third parties without first contacting our Legal Department so it can draft an appropriate nondisclosure agreement. Even after the agreement is signed, try only to accept as much information as is necessary to accomplish your business objectives. Also, please remember that you are personally responsible for reading the nondisclosure agreement and abiding by its restrictions.

You should also be sure that you obtain legal licenses for any third-party software you use in your work, and that you receive a publisher's consent or consult the Legal Department, before copying any publication or software in connection with your work with Google.

d. Competitors' Information

The level of business ethics to which we aspire requires that we apply the same rules to our competitors' information as we do to our own, and that we treat our competitors as we hope they will treat us. We respect our competitors and, above all else, believe in fair play in all circumstances; we would no sooner use a competitor's confidential information to our advantage than we would wish them to use ours. So, although gathering publicly available information about competitors is certainly a legitimate part of business competition, you should not seek out our competitors' confidential information or seek to use it if it comes into your possession. The same goes for confidential information belonging to any of your former employers. If an opportunity arises to take advantage of competitors' confidential information, remember: don't be evil. We compete, but we don't cheat.

e. Outside Communications

As a general rule, all Googlers know that we believe in being extremely careful about disclosing company information. It's almost always a bad idea to post discussions or information about Google on the Internet or anywhere else unless you're authorized to do so as part of your job. And you should never discuss the company with members of the media unless you've been explicitly authorized to do so by our public relations department.

V. Maintaining Books and Records

Accurate financial reporting is a core aspect of corporate professionalism. Our goal at Google is, and will always be, accounting transparency and accuracy.

To meet this standard, we consider it essential to maintain detailed, accurate books, records, and accounts to accurately reflect our transactions and to provide full, fair, accurate, timely, and understandable disclosure in reports and documents that we file with or submit to the Securities and Exchange Commission and in other public communications. To make sure that we get this right, Google maintains a system of internal accounting controls to reinforce and verify our own compliance with these policies.

Please be certain that, in the course of your work, you always stay in full compliance with any system of internal controls that is communicated to you by the CEO, CFO, General Counsel, Chief Compliance Officer, Finance Department, or head of your department, or that is generally communicated through the company's intranet site.

a. Business Transactions

Your own job at Google may or may not involve significant record-keeping; but whenever appropriate, we're all responsible for helping to make sure that Google's books are accurate. When you're involved in business transactions, be sure that you're following company procedures for carrying out and reporting them, obtaining appropriate management authorization for them (for instance, making sure you have Finance Department and, where appropriate, Legal Department approval before entering into revenue-related contracts), and maintaining appropriate documentation for them.

b. Reporting Procedures

Whenever the occasion arises, you should do everything possible to cooperate with our accounting/finance team, external auditors, and legal counsel by giving them candid, thorough information to ensure that our books and records are accurate. If your job calls it for it, you should make sure that you're fully familiar with Google's policies, such as our revenue recognition policy for the recording of sales and our purchasing policy for purchases, and that you report to the Finance Department any transactions of which you think they may not be aware.

c. Reporting Irregularities

Needless to say, you should never, ever in any way interfere with or seek to improperly influence, directly or indirectly, the auditing of Google's financial records; and you should never falsify any book, record or account, including time reports, expense accounts, and other personal Google records.

If in the course of your work you come to suspect accounting irregularities, no matter how small, you should immediately report them in accordance with our Reporting of Financial and Accounting Concerns Policy.

VI. Protecting Google's Assets

Google has (and intends to maintain) a well-earned reputation for generosity when it comes to employee benefits. But our long-term success will also depend on our ability to be smart about conserving company resources. Here are a few guidelines to follow in aiming to avoiding needless waste.

a. Company Equipment
Googlers should always take care to conserve company assets and equipment. All Google employees are provided with every possible tool we need to do our jobs effectively and comfortably, which makes it even more incumbent on all of us to avoid needless waste. Nobody's going to complain if you snag an extra bagel on Friday morning, but as a general rule, company funds, equipment, and other assets should not be requisitioned for purely personal use. If you aren't sure whether or not a given usage of company assets is okay, please ask your manager or Human Resources.

b. Computer and Other Communications Resources
Google's computer, telephony, and other communications resources are a crucial aspect of our company's property, both physical and intellectual. Please take all due care to maintain the security and privacy of these resources, and if you have any reason to believe that our network security has been violated — if, for instance, you have reason to believe that your network password may have been compromised — please promptly report the incident to the senior director of Information Services.

c. Need to Access and Monitor Communications on Google Facilities and Premises
From time to time, Google is required by law (for example, a subpoena or warrant) to monitor, access and disclose the contents of email, voicemail, computer files, other messages or files in transit or storage on our electronic facilities, and other materials on Google facilities or premises. In addition, Google has a strong interest in protecting its employees and users and maintaining the security of its resources and property. Consistent with that interest, Google reserves the right to monitor, access and disclose communications made on or information stored in any and all of its work areas, work product and equipment, including technological resources.

This means that Google cannot guarantee the confidentiality of personal materials stored on our systems or facilities, including personal communications made on Google's email or voicemail systems or personal materials stored physically or electronically on Google's premises or on computers on Google's premises. This also means that for legitimate business purposes (such as the need to access business records, to administer electronic facilities, to investigate suspected misconduct or to prevent misconduct from occurring), we monitor, access, and disclose information or communications, including personal information and communications, made or stored on Google facilities or premises. Finally, it goes without saying that misuse of company property or resources or any other misconduct discovered through monitoring, access or disclosure, regardless of the reason for the monitoring, access or disclosure, is a violation of this Code and is subject to appropriate disciplinary action, up to and including termination of employment.

d. Data Privacy

Google collects, stores, uses, and shares personal employee information from around the world. Use this data only in accordance with local data protection laws and Google's privacy policy.

e. Third-party Suppliers

As our company grows, we strike more and more deals with third-party suppliers of equipment and services — and we always strive to strike the best possible deal. If you're involved in selecting suppliers of goods or services, we strongly urge you to solicit competing bids to make sure that you're getting the best price. Still, price isn't the only factor worth considering; also take into account quality, service, and the terms and conditions of the proposed deal.

f. Company Contracts

Signing a contract on behalf of the company is a big deal. Please be sure never to enter into any contract unless you are authorized to do so (and if you are unsure if you are authorized, ask the Finance Department) and until it has been reviewed or approved as a form by the Legal Department. And even with these rules in mind, be careful never to sign a contract without first taking the time to study it yourself until you fully understand its terms.

VII. Obeying the Law

Google takes its responsibilities to comply with applicable laws and regulations very seriously. Although we recognize that it is probably impossible for you to understand all aspects of every applicable law, please take the time to familiarize yourself with the major laws and regulations that apply to your work and take advantage of our Legal Department to assist you and answer questions. We must all remember that our reputation is the foundation of our present and future success — and that earning, and maintaining, that reputation requires attention and effort to stay in compliance with the law.

a. Improper Payments
Payments made to corruptly influence the recipient or to otherwise gain an improper advantage in any situation are never acceptable at Google. Such improper payments not only expose Google to possible criminal prosecution but may also result in the prosecution of any employees who may have been involved in the making of any such payments. In fact, even offering to make such an improper payment may be a crime. Google expressly prohibits improper payments in all business dealings, in every country around the world, with both governments and the private sector. Improper payments should not be confused with reasonable and limited expenditures for gifts, business entertainment, and customer travel and living expenses directly related to the promotion of products or services or the execution of a contract. These payments are acceptable, subject to specific Google guidelines.

b. Export Controls
The United States is among a number of countries that maintain controls on the destinations to which products or software may be exported. The United States regulations are complex and apply both to exports from the United States and to exports of products from other countries, when those products contain components or technology of American origin. Software created in the United States is subject to these regulations even if it's duplicated and packaged abroad. In some circumstances, an oral presentation containing technical data made to foreign nationals in the United States may even constitute a controlled export.

The bottom line here is, if you're in any way involved in the exporting of Google products, services, software, or any form of technology to a foreign country or countries, or if you're considering beginning such a transaction, you should work with your manager to be absolutely certain that the transaction or transactions in question stay well within the bounds of U.S. law. If you and your manager aren't sure, please contact the Legal Department.

c. Antitrust Laws

Most countries have laws designed to encourage and protect free and fair competition. These laws often regulate a company's relationships with its distributors, resellers, dealers, partners, customers, and competitors. Generally speaking, these laws prohibit arrangements with competitors that restrain trade in some way, abuse intellectual property rights, or employ monopoly power, price discrimination, and other forms of unfair competition. Although the spirit of these laws, known as "antitrust," "competition," "consumer protection," or "unfair competition" laws, is straightforward, their application to particular situations can be quite complex. To ensure that Google complies fully with these laws, each of us should have a basic knowledge of them as they apply to our work, and should contact our Legal Department before questionable situations arise.

d. Insider Trading

In the course of your employment, you may learn of material information about Google or other companies before it is made public. You may simply overhear a hallway conversation or come across a memo left at a copy machine. Using this information for financial or other personal benefit or conveying this information to others constitutes a violation of this Code and may even violate the law. This includes buying or selling the securities of Google or any other company about which you have material non-public information or giving this "inside information" to anyone else who might use it to buy or sell securities.

VIII. Using Our Code

It's impossible to spell out every possible ethical scenario we Googlers might face, so we rely on one another's discretion and judgment to uphold this policy. We expect all Googlers to accept and be guided by both the letter and the spirit of this Code. Often this will mean making judgment calls about situations. When it comes to ethical conduct, we believe in erring on the side of caution, but not all violations are equally serious. That isn't an easy call, so if you aren't sure, by all means don't be afraid to ask questions of your manager or our Legal Department.

We should all consider it part of our job at Google not just to follow this Code but to help enforce it as well. If you know of a situation or incident that you feel may violate this Code, please report it to your manager or to Human Resources. Your report will be reviewed, and any Googler found to have violated any of the terms of this Code will be subject to disciplinary action, up to and including termination of employment. We'll also take any appropriate steps to prevent any further violations.

Finally, Google enforces a strict "no retaliation" policy. Retaliation for reporting a possible violation of this Code, otherwise making a complaint regarding a possible violation of this Code or participating in any investigation of a possible violation of this Code is strictly prohibited, If a complaint of retaliation is substantiated, appropriate disciplinary action will be taken, up to and including termination.

Google Code of Conduct © Google Inc. Used with permission.
http://investor.google.com/conduct.html